Birthday Cake, page 23

8-Layer Honey-Pistachio Cake, page 59

FAVORITE
CAKES

DEVELOPED BY

WILLIAMS SONOMA

TEST KITCHEN

Photographs **Sang An**

weldon**owen**

CONTENTS

Vanilla Ombré Layer Cake, page 57

Neapolitan "Ice Cream" Cake, page 64

MAKING GREAT CAKES

Nothing says celebration quite like a cake. For birthdays and holidays, family reunions, or just a fun weekend get-together with friends, cakes can be the main event or the grand finale. Whether it's a beginner-friendly lemony loaf cake flecked with poppy seeds, a classic and timeless vanilla layer cake, or a towering sponge cake covered with rich chocolate frosting, a homemade cake will make any gathering festive.

For some home bakers, even the simplest cake might seem intimidating. But we're here to help you master the basics. From prepping pans and whipping up the airiest batter to baking and decorating your masterpiece, the following pages guide you through invaluable cake-making how-tos, including an overview of ingredients and essential tools, frosting and piping techniques, and tips for troubleshooting your cakes to help ensure sweet success every time. We've organized our core cake and icing recipes in our Basic Recipes chapter, including buttery yellow and rich chocolate cakes and recipes for classic buttercreams and other frostings.

With these building blocks in hand, you'll be well prepared to try our recipes for the ultimate modern classics and specialty cakes that will inspire your creativity and evoke "oohs" and "aahs" from friends and family. A rainbow-speckled funfetti cake, Neapolitan ice cream cake, or a chocolate fox cake set the stage for a kid's birthday party, while a buttercream-covered pink ombré cake or a dulce de leche crepe cake are perfect for grown-up gatherings. Celebrate the winter holidays with a traditional bûche de noël or a festive gingerbread layer cake with maple-mascarpone whipped cream. And bring out contemporary classics, like brown butter and pineapple upside-down cake or a chocolate-hazelnut fallen cake, for a delectable finish to a dinner party or family gathering. No matter how you slice it, there's a cake for every season, every event, and every taste.

INGREDIENTS

There are many different types of cakes, from roulades and pound cakes to upside-down cakes, layer cakes, and cupcakes. Whatever their size and shape, most share common ingredients, including flour, sweetener, fat, and eggs.

FLOUR

Most cakes are made using all-purpose flour or cake flour. All-purpose flour is better for sturdier cakes that require the structure provided by the small amount of gluten it contains, whereas finely milled cake flour, which is lower in protein and gluten, is best for lighter, more delicate cakes. We've used all-purpose for the recipes in this book, but you can substitute 1 cup (4 oz/125 g) plus 2 tablespoons cake flour for every 1 cup (5 oz/155 g) all-purpose flour. Specialty flours, like almond flour, are ideal for tortes or other flourless cakes.

SUGAR

A cake isn't a cake without sugar or another sweetener! In its various forms, sugar lends both sweetness and moisture, helps keep cakes tender, and, when it caramelizes in the oven, gives baked goods a deliciously golden hue. White granulated sugar, light brown sugar, and confectioners' sugar are the most common types used in this book. Confectioners' sugar, also called powdered sugar, is very fine and ideal for frostings or as a sweetener for whipped cream.

BUTTER & OIL

Because they are fats, butter and oil deliver moisture, tenderness, and flavor to cakes. Choose a flavorless oil, such as canola or vegetable oil, unless a specialty version is required. Use unsalted butter because it allows you to control the amount of salt added, tends to be fresher, and lends a sweeter flavor to the finished cake. When whipped with sugar, butter keeps the crumb light and airy and even helps leaven a cake. When beaten into sweet meringue or with confectioners' sugar and other flavorings, butter creates silky rich frostings and buttercreams. To ensure a uniform mixture, let the butter soften to room temperature before beating.

EGGS

The egg is one of the most versatile ingredients in the baker's kitchen. Whipped egg whites add air and leavening to many cake batters or can be transformed into a meringue base for buttercream. Egg yolks are ideal for adding richness and for creating curds and custards used to fill cakes, while whole eggs lend structure to any baked good. The recipes in this book call for large eggs. For the freshest results, choose organic, pasture-raised eggs.

DAIRY

Dairy products like milk, buttermilk, and sour cream add richness, flavor, fat, and moisture to cakes. The recipes in this book use whole milk and full-fat sour cream for the best flavor. If you don't have buttermilk or sour cream, use plain whole-milk yogurt.

BAKING SODA & BAKING POWDER

Leavening is the result of gas bubbles expanding in the batter as it bakes, causing the cake to rise and lightening the texture and crumb. While some cakes are leavened purely with whipped egg whites, others include chemical leaveners, such as baking soda and baking powder. Baking soda must be used with another acidic ingredient in the batter, such as sour cream or lemon juice; it is activated when mixed with wet ingredients. Baking powder is a mixture of baking soda and a dry acid, like cream of tartar, and a little cornstarch. It's usually "double acting," meaning it is activated by both moisture and heat. You can substitute baking powder for baking soda but not vice versa.

FLAVORINGS

Chocolate and cocoa powder, vanilla extract or vanilla beans, citrus zest, liqueurs and other extracts, and countless spices like cinnamon and nutmeg can help shape the personality of your finished creation.

Champagne & Raspberry Mini Layer Cakes, page 24

ESSENTIAL TOOLS

Using proper cake-making tools ensures the best results and gives your cakes a polished appearance. Here are the indispensable tools that help you beat batters easily, whip up the fluffiest frostings, and create professional-style decorations.

ELECTRIC MIXER

An electric stand mixer will help you make cakes, fillings, and frostings with ease. While some batters can be prepared with just a bowl and a wooden spoon or a handheld whisk, you'll find it far easier to whip egg whites and whole eggs and to cream butter and sugar with a sturdy tabletop mixer. There are two commonly used attachments for a stand mixer: the paddle, also called the flat beater, which is ideal for creaming butter and sugar and beating batters, and the whisk or whip attachment, which aerates egg whites, whole eggs, and cream. Handheld mixers will also work, although they lack the power of a stand mixer and often cannot beat thick or sturdy batters.

CAKE PANS

Different cakes require different types and sizes of pans. Whatever pan you use, be sure to prep it as directed in your recipe before making the batter, as it will need to go in the oven immediately. For most cake pans, choose ones made from sturdy, heavy-duty aluminum.

Round cake pans: Most of the layer cake recipes in this book call for two round 8- or 9-inch (20- to 23-cm) cake pans that are 2 inches (5 cm) high. Avoid nonstick pans when baking sponge cakes, which need an ungreased surface in order to rise high.

Muffin pans: Standard-sized or mini, a muffin pan can be greased or lined with paper cupcake liners for cupcakes, tea cakes, and other mini or bite-sized cakes.

Specialty pans: Angel food and chiffon cakes are traditionally made in a tall, 10-inch (25-cm) diameter footed tube pan with a removable base. A Bundt pan is a popular ring-shaped pan that gives cakes a distinctive scalloped or patterned look; they range in size from mini to extra large, but 12-cup (3-l)

pans are the most common. A springform pan features a spring-loaded latch that tightens a collar around a removable base; these are great for tall cakes, coffee cakes, and cheesecakes. Sheet cakes and roulades, or rolled cakes, are typically baked in a 12-by-16-inch (30-by-40-cm) sheet cake pan (also called a half sheet pan or rimmed baking sheet) with 1-inch (2.5-cm) sides.

SPATULAS

A heatproof silicone rubber spatula is great for stirring cake batter, scraping it out of the bowl and into the cake pan, and spreading it evenly before baking. An offset spatula, which features a stiff metal blade that is bent near the handle, facilitates moving cake layers from wire cooling racks to a cake stand or platter, and is useful for spreading fillings and frostings. Mini versions are perfect for smaller cakes. An icing spatula has a long, straight blade and is also excellent for spreading fillings and frostings.

SIFTER

Sifting dry ingredients, such as flour, baking powder or baking soda, cocoa, and confectioners' sugar, lightens them so that they don't deflate any whipped ingredients into which you fold them. Sifting also removes any lumps, particularly in fine dry ingredients that tend to clump, including cake flour, cocoa, and confectioners' sugar. Choose a fine-mesh sifter or sieve for best results.

PASTRY BAGS & TIPS

Made from washable canvas, silicone, or plastic, a pastry bag is useful when dividing small amounts of batter, filling the layers between cake, and putting the final decorative touches on your masterpiece. A set of plain and star tips will enable you to frost and decorate with professional finesse.

CAKE TIPS & TECHNIQUES

Creating a showstopping cake starts with making sure it bakes correctly and comes out of the pan without a hitch. Here are prepping, mixing, and piping techniques every baker should know.

CUTTING PARCHMENT ROUNDS

To line a cake pan with parchment paper, tear off a piece of parchment paper that is slightly larger than the pan's diameter. Place the cake pan right side up on the parchment and use a pencil to trace the pan's circumference onto the paper. Cut out the circle just slightly inside the traced circle (or square) so that the parchment fits snugly in the pan and doesn't fold up the pan's sides. If you're using several pans, make one for each pan.

GREASING A CAKE PAN

If your recipe calls for buttering and flouring your cake pan, make sure you prep the pan before you make the batter. Unless noted otherwise, cake pans may be prepared as follows:

• To grease the pan, spread about ½ tablespoon unsalted butter into a thin even layer all over the inside of the pan or coat with a thin layer of cooking spray.

• Line the bottom of the pan with a parchment round (see above) and lightly butter the top of the parchment.

• Add 1 tablespoon flour to the pan and, holding the pan over your work surface, rotate the pan so that the flour sticks to the butter all over the inside of the pan.

• Tap the pan, bottom side up, on the work surface to dislodge any excess flour and use the excess in a second pan or discard.

FOLDING IN INGREDIENTS

To fold whipped egg whites (or whipped cream) into a batter, you want to retain as much aeration as possible, so use a gentle hand and as few strokes as possible. With a large rubber spatula, dollop a scoop of the whipped egg whites onto the batter, then gently stir it in; this step lightens the batter to make it easier for folding. Spoon the remaining egg whites onto the batter. Starting in the center of the bowl, use the rubber spatula to "slice" through the whites and batter to the bottom of the bowl, then pull the spatula up the side of the bowl and swoop over the top and back to the middle. This action will gently mix the egg whites and batter together. Continue with this motion, rotating the bowl, until the mixture is combined and no white streaks are visible, being careful not to overmix and lose the aeration.

ASSEMBLING CAKE LAYERS

Removing the cake from the pan:

• Let the cake cool in the pan on a wire rack for about 10 minutes before removing it; this will help prevent the cake from sticking to the pan.

• If making a cake in an ungreased pan (such as chiffon or genoise), run a thin paring knife around the inside edge to release the cake.

• Place the wire rack upside down over the cake pan and invert the rack and pan together. Carefully remove the pan and any parchment lining. Repeat with the remaining cake layer(s). Let the cakes cool completely before proceeding.

Slicing a cake into layers:

• Place the cooled cake on a flat surface; a revolving cake-decorating stand is ideal.

• Hold a ruler up to the side of the cake and mark the midpoint (or where you'd like to slice it) with toothpicks at regular intervals around the cake.

• Using a long serrated knife and a sawing motion, slowly cut the cake where it is marked, rotating as you cut and working your way to the center of the cake.

• Slide the top layer onto a cardboard cake circle or other flat surface.

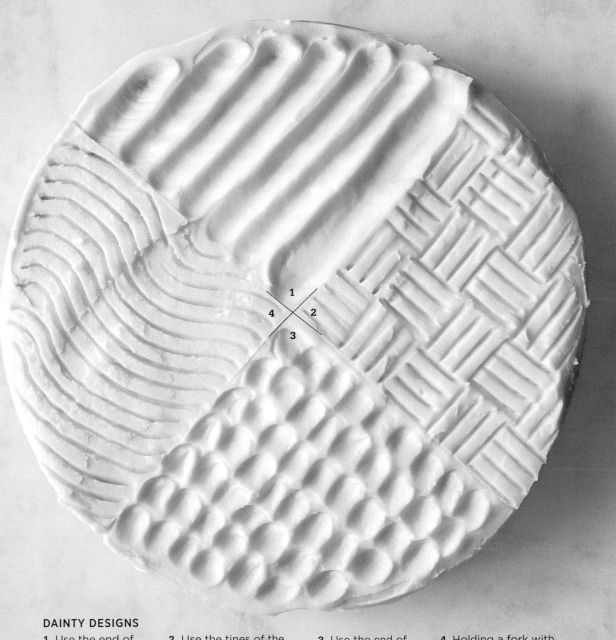

DAINTY DESIGNS

1 Use the end of a wooden spoon to draw lines through the buttercream.

2 Use the tines of the back of a fork to create a basket-weave pattern. Start in the center and turn the fork 45 degrees each time you press it into the frosting.

3 Use the end of a wooden spoon to press a pattern into the cake.

4 Holding a fork with the tines pointing straight down, use the tines to draw squiggly lines through the buttercream.

PIPING GUIDE

With a little practice, you can become a piping pro. A coupler will let you switch out different tips on your pastry bag with ease.

Use round tips for outlining and filling, making dots, stems, flower centers, lattices, and lace.

Use an open-star tip for creating textured round borders and drop flowers.

Use a closed-star tip for making zigzags, stars, shells, rosettes, and scrolls.

Use a basket-weave tip for designing smooth or ribbed strips and texture.

FILL THE CAKE LAYERS

- Place the bottom cake layer on a cardboard cake circle atop a work surface or on a revolving cake-decorating stand.

- Using a pastry brush, brush away any crumbs.

- Mound the specifed amount of filling onto the center of the cake, then use an icing spatula to evenly spread the filling to the edges. The type of filling and the thickness of the cake will determine the thickness of the filling layer: jam should be thin, curd and frosting should be thicker. If you want to use a pastry bag to pipe the frosting, see the how-to photos on pages 16–17.

- Top the filling with the next cake layer, placing it cut side up. Do not spread filling on the top layer unless directed in the recipe.

FROST THE CAKE

Follow these steps when frosting a round or square layer cake.

- Place the filled layer cake on a work surface or on a revolving cake-decorating stand. Using an icing spatula, spread a very thin layer of frosting over the top and sides of the cake. This is called the crumb coat. Refrigerate for about 20 minutes to allow the frosting to firm up. This step will ensure that loose crumbs do not invade your final layer of frosting.

- Place the cake on a serving plate or on a revolving cake-decorating stand. Cut 4 strips of parchment paper and tuck them around the cake bottom to protect the surface from drips.

- Set aside a portion of the frosting for decorating and piping, if desired.

- Using an icing spatula, spread a mound of frosting evenly over the top of the cake. Be careful not to lift the icing spatula directly up or you might tear the cake.

- Using the back of the icing spatula, spread the frosting evenly over the sides of the cake, smoothing it gently.

- If you do encounter crumbs, wipe them away from the frosting before adding more frosting to the cake.

- Dip the icing spatula in hot water and wipe dry. Hold the spatula parallel to the side of the cake and smooth the frosting around the entire cake. Wipe the spatula clean, then rewarm it in the water and wipe dry.

- Hold the spatula parallel to the top of the cake and swipe it across the top from the edge to smooth the edges, while rotating the cake.

- The cake is now ready to be piped with frosting and decorated as desired.

- When you have finished frosting and decorating the cake, remove the parchment strips.

TO MAKE A "NAKED" CAKE

- Be sure to grease your cake pans well to keep your layers neat. Use a pastry brush to brush away any crumbs as you work.

- Stack and fill your cake layers with frosting, using a piping bag to pipe the frosting neatly around the edges.

- Chill the filled layered cake until the frosting hardens. You can then frost the top and add decorations, or take it a step further.

- Spread a layer of frosting over the top, then spread a thin layer down the sides. Use the edge of a metal frosting spatula, an offset spatula, or a metal bench scraper to scrape away enough of the frosting so that you can see the cake layers underneath. Chill until the frosting hardens, then decorate the top.

STORING CAKES

To store an uncut and unfrosted cake, wrap the cake tightly in plastic wrap so that the plastic is touching the top, sides, and bottom. The cake can be stored at room temperature for 2–3 days.

To store a frosted but uncut cake, cover the cake with a cake dome or a large bowl and store at room temperature for 2–3 days.

To store a frosted and cut cake, press a piece of plastic wrap against the cut area, then cover with a cake dome or large bowl and store at room temperature for 2–3 days.

1

Use a pastry bag fitted with a large round tip to pipe a border around the edge of the first cake layer.

2

Fill in the center of the layer using a zigzag pattern.

5

Pipe a border around the edge of the second cake layer.

6

Repeat the process of piping and spreading the filling over the center of the second layer.

3

Use a small offset spatula to spread the filling over the first cake layer.

4

Add the next layer to the top of the cake.

7

Add the third layer to the top of the cake.

8

Use a large offset spatula to create a crumb coat around the outside of the cake.

TROUBLESHOOTING

Sometimes, despite our best efforts, a cake simply doesn't turn out in the way we would like. Here is a list of the most common problems we encountered when testing the recipes for this book, and the best ways to solve them so your next cake will bake to perfection.

BURNT TOP

Loosely drape aluminum foil over the top of the cake if it begins to overbrown during baking. If the cake overbrowns despite your best efforts, use a long serrated knife to trim the burnt area from the top of the cake and discard.

NOT RISING

Use an oven thermometer to check that your oven's temperature is accurate. If the oven is too cool, your cake will not rise properly.

Make sure that you added the leavening or that it isn't out of date. But don't toss out a poorly risen cake! Cut it into chunks and use it for a trifle (a layered dessert with cake, sherry, custard, fruit, and whipped cream).

SHRINKING FROM PAN SIDES

This can happen for a number of reasons:
• Overmixing the batter—be careful not to overmix the batter, especially when folding in aerated ingredients.
• Too much leavener—be sure to use level teaspoons, not heaping ones.
• Inaccurate oven temperature—check temperature with an oven thermometer, and take care not to overbake the cake.
• Overgreasing the pan—a thin layer of butter or cooking oil spray, and sometimes another of flour, helps prevent cakes from sticking to the pan.

AIR POCKETS

Once you spread the batter in the cake pan, gently tap the pan on the counter to release any air pockets. Alternatively, drag a wooden skewer through the batter.

OVERMIXED OR UNDERMIXED BATTER

Overmixed cake batter will result in a heavy, dense cake. Stop mixing just when you see that the ingredients are evenly blended and you can no longer see streaks of individual ingredients. Undermixing can produce a lumpy cake or one with streaks of ingredients that are visible after baking; be sure that you mix the ingredients thoroughly but then stop.

One last suggestion: Enjoy! Baking a cake is fun, and even if your cake turns out a bit lopsided or unevenly frosted, it will still taste heavenly. Practice makes perfect, and as you spend more time baking cakes you will master all of the techniques described in the following pages and reap the reward—a delicious, beautiful homemade cake to share with family and friends.

Angel Food Cake with Minted Strawberries
& Mascarpone Cream, page 38

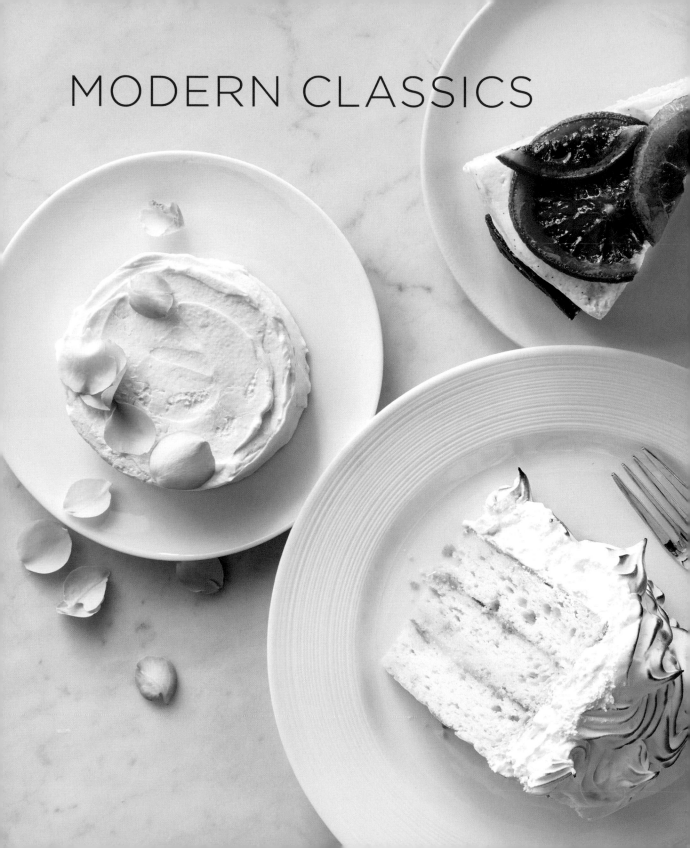

MODERN CLASSICS

KIDS AT HEART
Adults will love this festive celebration cake just as much as little ones do.

This cheerful, rainbow-speckled layer cake is the perfect finale for any kid's birthday party. All you need to transform a buttery yellow cake into a colorful showstopper is a handful of rainbow nonpareils or sprinkles. The marzipan is easy to prepare and cut into fun shapes, but if you want to keep things simple, just decorate the buttercream with more rainbow sprinkles!

BIRTHDAY CAKE

1 recipe Marzipan (page 90; made with food colorings of your choice)

1 recipe Yellow Cake (page 94)

1 cup (5 oz/160 g) wax-coated rainbow sprinkles, plus more for decorating

1 recipe Quick Vanilla Buttercream (page 97)

Serves 12

Make the marzipan and refrigerate as directed.

Preheat the oven, prepare the pans, and make the yellow cake batter as directed. Remove the bowl from the mixer and, using a rubber spatula, fold in the sprinkles.

Divide the batter evenly between the prepared pans and spread evenly. Bake until a toothpick inserted into the center of the cakes comes out clean, about 55 minutes. Transfer the pans to wire racks and let cool for 10 minutes, then invert the cakes onto the racks and let cool completely.

Roll out the marzipan dough ½ inch (12 mm) thick and cut out triangles. Make the quick vanilla buttercream.

To assemble the cake, using a large serrated knife, cut each cake in half horizontally to create 4 thin layers. Place the bottom layer cut side down on a cake stand or serving plate. Using an offset spatula, spread about one-fourth of the buttercream evenly over the cake. Repeat with the remaining layers. Spread the top and sides of the cake with a very thin layer of buttercream and refrigerate for 30 minutes. Spread the remaining buttercream over the top and sides of the chilled cake. Cover the entire top of the cake with sprinkles. Arrange the marzipan triangles next to each other around the sides of the cake to form a banner, pressing gently to adhere. Cut into slices and serve.

TIP *For an exceptionally colorful cake, use small pearled sprinkles. For a more controlled speckled effect, use sprinkles like those you'd find in an ice cream shop.*

These elegant layer cakes shine with the addition of sparkling wine and raspberry purée. There's no need to use expensive champagne, but use a sparkling wine that you'd like to drink and serve glasses of it alongside the cakes.

CHAMPAGNE & RASPBERRY MINI LAYER CAKES

Unsalted butter, for greasing

All-purpose flour, for dusting

1 recipe Champagne Cake (page 92)

½ recipe Raspberry Filling (page 103)

FOR THE CHAMPAGNE BUTTERCREAM

1 cup (8 oz/250 g) unsalted butter, at room temperature

4 cups (1 lb/500 g) confectioners' sugar

5 tablespoons (80 ml) sparkling wine

1 teaspoon pure vanilla extract

¼ teaspoon kosher salt

⅓ cup (1 oz/20 g) freeze-dried raspberries

⅓ cup (1½ oz/45 g) fresh raspberries

Serves 6; makes three 3-inch (7.5-cm) 3-layer cakes

Preheat the oven to 350°F (180°C). Grease a rimmed sheet cake pan, line the pan with parchment paper, then grease the parchment. Dust with flour, then tap out any excess. Make the champagne cake batter.

Spread the batter in the prepared pan. Bake until a toothpick inserted into the center of the cake comes out clean, about 25 minutes. Let cool completely in the pan on a wire rack, then invert the cake onto a cutting board or an upside-down baking sheet. Remove the parchment. Using a 3-inch (7.5-cm) round cutter, cut out 9 rounds.

Make the raspberry filling.

To make the buttercream, in the bowl of a stand mixer fitted with the paddle attachment, beat the butter on medium speed until smooth, about 2 minutes. Add the confectioners' sugar, sparkling wine, vanilla, and salt, raise the speed to medium-high, and beat until combined, stopping the mixer to scrape down the sides of the bowl as needed.

To assemble the cakes, transfer one-fourth of the buttercream to a pastry bag and cut a ½-inch (12-mm) opening. Pipe a ring around the outside edge of 1 cake round, then spread a layer of raspberry filling in the center (see p.15). Top with another cake round and repeat to form 3 cake layers. Repeat to assemble the remaining cakes.

Refrigerate the cakes until set, about 1 hour. Spread the remaining buttercream over the tops and sides of the cakes. Garnish with freeze-dried and fresh raspberries and serve.

TIP *If the buttercream is too loose, add more confectioners' sugar. If it is too thick, stir in more sparkling wine or a few teaspoons of milk.*

STAR OF THE PARTY
These pretty mini cakes are a welcome guest at an afternoon tea party, bridal shower, or any fancy fête.

Topping this moist lemon and almond pound cake with thin slices of lemon, then drizzling it with yogurt-spiked icing and plenty of toasted almond slices, results in the ultimate loaf cake. Serve with a steaming cup of tea for an afternoon treat.

LEMON POPPY SEED LOAF CAKE WITH ALMOND ICING

FOR THE CAKE

¾ cup (6 oz/185 g) unsalted butter, at room temperature, plus more for greasing

1¾ cups (9 oz/280 g) all-purpose flour, plus more for dusting

2 teaspoons baking powder

½ teaspoon *each* baking soda and kosher salt

1 cup (8 oz/250 g) granulated sugar

3 large eggs

2 teaspoons grated lemon zest

¼ cup (60 ml) fresh lemon juice

½ teaspoon almond extract

½ cup (125 ml) buttermilk

2 tablespoons poppy seeds

1 lemon, thinly sliced

FOR THE ALMOND ICING

½ cup (2 oz/60 g) confectioners' sugar

1 tablespoon 2% Greek yogurt

¼ teaspoon almond extract

⅛ teaspoon pure vanilla extract

Toasted slivered almonds, for garnish

Serves 9

To make the cake, preheat the oven to 350°F (180°C). Grease a 9-by-5-inch (23-by-13-cm) loaf pan and dust with flour, then tap out any excess.

In a bowl, sift together the flour, baking powder, baking soda, and salt. Set aside.

In the bowl of a stand mixer fitted with the paddle attachment, beat together the butter and granulated sugar on medium speed until light and fluffy, about 2 minutes. Add the eggs one at a time and beat until incorporated, then add the lemon zest and juice and almond extract and beat until smooth, about 1 minute. Reduce the speed to low and add the flour mixture in 2 additions, alternating with the buttermilk and beginning and ending with the flour, and beat just until the flour disappears. Sprinkle in the poppy seeds and beat until evenly distributed, about 30 seconds.

Pour the batter into the prepared pan and spread evenly. Arrange the lemon slices on top in rows of three, slightly overlapping the slices. Bake until the edges of the cake are golden brown and a toothpick inserted into the center comes out clean, 55–60 minutes. Transfer the pan to a wire rack and let cool for 15 minutes, then invert the cake onto the rack and let cool completely.

To make the icing, in a small bowl, whisk together the confectioners' sugar, yogurt, almond and vanilla extracts, and 1 teaspoon water. Spoon the icing over the top of the cooled cake. Using a pastry brush, smooth the icing and allow the lemon slices to peek through. Sprinkle with the almonds and serve.

The tart-sweet raspberry core of these delicate white cupcakes makes for a stunning and delicious contrast. Topped with silky white chocolate buttercream and a sprinkle of freeze-dried raspberries, these little cakes are instantly elevated to party status.

VANILLA CUPCAKES WITH RASPBERRIES & WHITE CHOCOLATE

1 recipe White Cake (page 92)

1 recipe Raspberry Filling (page 103)

FOR THE WHITE CHOCOLATE BUTTERCREAM

2 cups (1 lb/500 g) unsalted butter, at room temperature

1½ lb (750 g) white chocolate, melted and cooled slightly

2 cups (8 oz/250 g) confectioners' sugar

¼ teaspoon kosher salt

1 cup (3 oz/60 g) freeze-dried raspberries, lightly crushed

Makes 24 cupcakes

Place 1 rack in the upper third and 1 rack in the lower third of the oven and preheat to 350°F (180°C). Line 24 standard muffin cups with paper liners.

Make the white cake batter.

Divide the batter among the prepared muffin cups, filling them about two-thirds full and spread evenly. Bake until the tops of the cupcakes spring back when lightly touched and a toothpick inserted into the center comes out clean, 25–30 minutes, rotating the pans between the racks halfway through baking. Transfer the pans to wire racks and let cool for 10 minutes, then remove the cupcakes from the pans and let cool completely on the racks.

Make the raspberry filling. Set aside.

To make the buttercream, in the bowl of a stand mixer fitted with the paddle attachment, beat the butter on medium speed until smooth, about 2 minutes. Reduce the speed to low, drizzle in the melted white chocolate, and beat until combined. Add the confectioners' sugar and salt, raise the speed to medium-high, and beat until light and fluffy, about 2 minutes.

Using a melon baller, spoon, or small paring knife, gently scoop or cut out the center of each cupcake from the top and reserve the cake tops. Spoon a heaping 1 teaspoon raspberry filling into the center of each cupcake, then cover with a reserved cake top. Spread the buttercream over the cupcakes. Sprinkle with the freeze-dried raspberries and serve.

FINISHING TOUCH
The "naked cake" effect on this modern carrot cake sets it apart from a more traditional presentation.

Take classic carrot cake to the next level by transforming it into a triple-layer treat made moist with crushed pineapple, then embellished with cream cheese frosting with toasty walnuts. Using real carrots "buried" in the frosting is an easy way to add a bit of whimsy to the decoration.

CARROT CAKE WITH CREAM CHEESE FROSTING

FOR THE CAKE

¾ cup (180 ml) canola oil, plus more for greasing

2¼ cups (11½ oz/360 g) all-purpose flour, plus more for dusting

2 teaspoons baking soda

2 teaspoons kosher salt

5 teaspoons ground cinnamon

2 teaspoons ground ginger

¼ teaspoon ground nutmeg

⅛ teaspoon ground cloves

3 large eggs

2¼ cups (18 oz/560 g) sugar

¾ cup (180 ml) buttermilk

2 teaspoons pure vanilla extract

6 oz (185 g) crushed pineapple, drained

3 cups (15 oz/470 g) grated peeled carrots

1 recipe Cream Cheese Frosting (page 101)

3 carrots, with tops attached

½ cup (2 oz/60 g) chopped toasted walnuts

Serves 16

To make the cake, preheat the oven to 350°F (180°C). Grease three 9-inch (23-cm) round cake pans, line the bottoms of the pans with parchment paper, then grease the parchment. Dust with flour, then tap out any excess.

In a large bowl, sift together the flour, baking soda, salt, cinnamon, ginger, nutmeg, and cloves. Set aside.

In the bowl of a stand mixer fitted with the paddle attachment, beat together the eggs, sugar, oil, buttermilk, and vanilla on low speed until smooth, about 1 minute. Add the flour mixture in 2 additions and beat until combined, about 1 minute. Add the pineapple and grated carrots and beat until just incorporated.

Divide the batter evenly among the prepared pans and spread evenly. Bake until the tops of the cakes are browned and shiny and a toothpick inserted into the center comes out clean, 25–30 minutes. Transfer the pans to wire racks and let cool for 10 minutes, then invert the cakes onto the racks and let cool completely.

Make the cream cheese frosting.

To assemble the cake, place 1 cake layer on a cake stand or serving plate. Spread one-third of the cream cheese frosting evenly over the cake. Repeat with the remaining cake layers, including the top layer. Using an offset spatula, spread a thin layer of frosting on all sides of the cake to create a "naked" cake effect. Carefully peel the carrots, keeping the tops intact. Gently press the carrots onto the top of the cake in varying heights. Scatter the walnuts around the carrots and serve.

A scant amount of fragrant rosewater and two kinds of vanilla add sophistication to these dainty individual cakes. Fresh or dried rose petals make a gorgeous garnish, especially if you use a variety of hues. Use only those you know to be pesticide-free.

ROSE & VANILLA BEAN MINI TEA CAKES

Unsalted butter, for greasing

All-purpose flour, for dusting

1 recipe White Cake (page 92)

1 vanilla bean, split and seeds scraped, seeds reserved

1 recipe Traditional Vanilla Buttercream (page 97)

1 teaspoon pure vanilla extract

1 tablespoon rose water or ½ teaspoon rose extract

2 drops red food coloring, plus more as needed (optional)

Fresh or dried rose petals, for garnish

Serves 12; makes twelve 3-inch (7.5-cm) tea cakes

Preheat the oven to 350°F (180°C). Grease a rimmed sheet cake pan, line the pan with parchment paper, then grease the parchment. Dust with flour, then tap out any excess.

Make the white cake batter, adding the vanilla bean seeds along with the vanilla extract.

Transfer the batter to the prepared sheet pan and spread evenly. Bake until a toothpick inserted into the center of the cake comes out clean, about 25 minutes. Transfer the pan to a wire rack and let the cake cool completely in the pan, then invert the cake onto a cutting board or onto an upside-down baking sheet. Remove the parchment paper. Using a 3-inch (7.5-cm) round cutter, cut out 12 rounds. Set aside.

Make the traditional vanilla buttercream, adding the rose water when you add the vanilla extract and begin beating the egg whites with the stand mixer. After beating in all of the butter, add the food coloring, if using, and beat until completely incorporated, adding more food coloring as desired.

Spread the top of each tea cake with a ¼-inch (6-mm) layer of the buttercream, using an offset spatula to smooth the sides. Garnish with the rose petals and serve.

BEAUTIFUL BLOOMS
Create a dramatic presentation by displaying these elegant mini cakes on a tiered stand.

HIDDEN FLAVORS

A combination of coconut milk and extract transform traditional buttercream for this chic celebration cake.

Coconut layer cake, split and filled with lemon or lime curd and slathered with fluffy 7-minute frosting and a blizzard of shredded coconut, is a mainstay of the Southern kitchen. We've updated this classic with our moist buttermilk cake, homemade lime curd, and coconut buttercream, topped with a flurry of colorful flowers and finely grated lime zest.

COCONUT & LIME CURD LAYER CAKE

1 recipe Lime Curd (page 90)

1 recipe Coconut Buttercream (page 98)

FOR THE CAKE

1 cup (8 oz/250 g) plus 2 tablespoons unsalted butter, at room temperature, plus more for greasing

4 cups (1¼ lb/625 g) plus 2 tablespoons all-purpose flour, plus more for dusting

3 ¾ teaspoons baking powder

1⅛ teaspoons baking soda

1⅛ teaspoons kosher salt

4 large egg whites plus 2 large eggs

3 cups (1½ lb/750 g) sugar

1½ tablespoons pure vanilla extract

2¼ cups (560 ml) buttermilk

Edible flowers and grated lime zest, for garnish

Serves 18

Make the lime curd and coconut buttercream. Cover and refrigerate until ready to use or for up to three days.

To make the cake, preheat the oven to 350°F (180°C). Grease three 8-inch (20-cm) round cake pans, line the bottoms of the pans with parchment paper, then grease the parchment. Dust with flour, then tap out any excess.

In a bowl, sift together the flour, baking powder, baking soda, and salt. Set aside.

In the bowl of the stand mixer fitted with the whisk attachment, beat together the egg whites and 1 cup (8 oz/250 g) of the sugar on medium-high speed until soft peaks form, about 5 minutes. Set aside.

In the clean bowl of the stand mixer fitted with the paddle attachment, beat together the butter and the remaining 2 cups (1 lb/500 g) sugar on medium speed until light and fluffy, about 2 minutes. Add the eggs one at a time and vanilla and beat until incorporated, about 1 minute. Stop the mixer and scrape down the sides of the bowl. With the mixer on low speed, add the flour mixture in 3 additions, alternating with the buttermilk and beginning and ending with the flour and beat until combined. Stop the mixer and scrape down the sides of the bowl. Raise the speed to high and beat for 20 seconds.

Continued on page 34

Continued from page 33

COCONUT & LIME CURD LAYER CAKE

Using a rubber spatula, gently fold the egg whites into the butter mixture until completely incorporated, taking care not to deflate the peaks.

Divide the batter evenly among the prepared pans and spread evenly. Bake until a toothpick inserted into the center of the cakes comes out clean, 40–45 minutes. Transfer the pans to wire racks and let cool for 10 minutes, then invert the cakes onto the racks and let cool completely.

Transfer one-fourth of the buttercream to a pastry bag and cut a ½-inch (12-mm) opening.

To assemble the cake, place 1 cake layer, top side up, on a cake stand or serving plate. Pipe a ring of buttercream around the edge of the cake, then fill the center with half of the lime curd. Top with a second cake layer, pipe a ring of buttercream, and fill the center with the remaining lime curd. Top with the third cake layer and spread the remaining buttercream over the top. If desired, reserve a small amount of buttercream and spread a thin layer on the sides to create a "naked" cake effect.

Garnish the cake with edible flowers and lime zest and serve.

TIP *For thinner layers, you can make a single batch of the White Cake (page 92) and divide it evenly among three pans.*

Red velvet cake originally got its name from the moist, velvety texture and subtle red hue created by the reaction between buttermilk, cocoa powder, and vinegar. For a kid's birthday party, decorate the cake with rainbow sprinkles on top of the cake and colorful marzipan shapes around the base.

RED VELVET CAKE WITH CREAM CHEESE FROSTING

½ cup (4 oz/125 g) unsalted butter, at room temperature, plus more for greasing

2½ cups (12½ oz/390 g) all-purpose flour, plus more for dusting

¼ cup (¾ oz/20 g) unsweetened cocoa powder

1 teaspoon *each* baking powder and kosher salt

1½ cups (375 ml) buttermilk

2 tablespoons red food coloring

2 cups (1 lb/500 g) sugar

2 large eggs

2 teaspoons pure vanilla extract

1½ teaspoons baking soda

1 tablespoon distilled white vinegar

1 recipe Cream Cheese Frosting (page 101)

Serves 12

Preheat the oven to 350°F (180°C). Grease two 8-inch (20-cm) round cake pans, line the bottoms of the pans with parchment paper, then grease the parchment. Dust with flour, then tap out any excess.

In a bowl, sift together the flour, cocoa powder, baking powder, and salt. In a small bowl, whisk together the buttermilk and food coloring. Set aside.

In the bowl of a stand mixer fitted with the paddle attachment, beat together the butter and sugar on medium speed until light and fluffy, about 2 minutes. Add the eggs one at a time and then the vanilla and beat until incorporated, about 1 minute. Reduce the speed to low and add the flour mixture in 3 additions, alternating with the buttermilk and beginning and ending with the flour, and beat until combined. In a small bowl, whisk together the baking soda and vinegar. When the fizzing subsides, use a rubber spatula to fold it into the batter.

Divide the batter evenly between the prepared pans. Bake until a toothpick inserted into the center of the cakes comes out clean, 35–40 minutes. Transfer the pans to wire racks and let cool for 10 minutes, then invert the cakes onto the racks and let cool completely.

Make the cream cheese frosting. To assemble the cake, place 1 cake layer on a serving plate. Spread about one-third of the frosting onto the top of the cake and spread evenly with an offset spatula. Place the other layer on top. Cover the entire cake with a thin layer of frosting and refrigerate for 30 minutes. Working with the chilled cake, spread the remaining cream cheese frosting on the top and sides of the cake.

CARAMEL INFUSION
Tequila punches up the decadent caramel drizzled over this moist cake.

Tres leches gets its name from the triple mix of spice-infused sweet condensed milk, rich evaporated milk, and heavy cream that is poured over the just-baked cake. To maximize the flavor, prepare the cake with its cloak of fragrant milk, then let stand overnight before serving.

TRES LECHES CAKE

FOR THE CAKE

Nonstick cooking spray for greasing

1½ cups (7½ oz/235 g) all-purpose flour

2 teaspoons baking powder

¼ teaspoon kosher salt

3 large eggs, separated

1½ cups (12 oz/375 g) granulated sugar

2 teaspoons pure vanilla extract

½ cup (125 ml) whole milk

1 cup (250 ml) heavy cream

1 cinnamon stick

5 whole cloves

1 can (14 oz/440 g) condensed sweetened milk

1 can (12 fl oz/375 ml) evaporated milk

1 recipe Tequila Caramel Sauce (page 103)

2 recipes Classic Whipped Cream (page 91)

Serves 24

To make the cake, preheat the oven to 350°F (180°C). Grease a 9-by-13-inch (23-by-33-cm) baking pan, line the bottom of the pan with parchment paper, then grease the parchment. In a bowl, whisk together the flour, baking powder, and salt. Set aside.

In the bowl of a stand mixer fitted with the whisk attachment, beat together the egg whites and granulated sugar on medium-high speed until stiff peaks form, about 4 minutes. Add the egg yolks one at a time, beating until incorporated after each addition, then beat in the vanilla. Reduce the speed, add the flour mixture in 3 additions, alternating with the whole milk and beginning and ending with the flour, until blended. Raise the speed to high and beat for 30 seconds.

Transfer the batter to the prepared pan and spread evenly. Bake until a toothpick inserted into the center comes out clean, about 30 minutes. Transfer the pan to a wire rack and let cool for 10 minutes, then invert the cake onto the rack and pierce all over with a fork.

Meanwhile, in a small saucepan over medium-high heat, combine the cream, cinnamon stick, and cloves and bring to a simmer. Remove from the heat and let cool to room temperature. Remove and discard the cinnamon stick and cloves. Transfer the cream to a bowl and whisk in the condensed milk and evaporated milk. Slowly pour the spiced cream mixture over the warm cake, allowing the cream to soak in before pouring more. Cover the cake with plastic wrap and refrigerate overnight.

Just before serving, make the caramel sauce and whipped cream. Spread a layer of the caramel over the cake's top. Spread the whipped cream over the caramel, drizzle with more caramel, and serve.

Light and delicate, a towering angel food cake is an ode to the airy effect of whipped egg whites. A thick slice served with fresh fruit and whipped cream is always a favorite, but take it up a notch with macerated strawberries, fresh mint, and rich mascarpone whipped cream, for a perfect contrast to the pillowy cake.

ANGEL FOOD CAKE WITH MINTED STRAWBERRIES & MASCARPONE CREAM

FOR THE CAKE

1 cup (5 oz/155 g) all-purpose flour

1½ cups (12 oz/375 g) sugar

12 large egg whites

½ teaspoon kosher salt

1 teaspoon cream of tartar

2 teaspoons pure vanilla extract

FOR THE MINTED STRAWBERRIES

1 lb (500 g) strawberries, hulled and quartered

¼ cup (2 oz/60 g) sugar

1 tablespoon chopped fresh mint, plus whole leaves for garnish

1 recipe Mascarpone Whipped Cream (page 91)

Serves 12–15

Preheat the oven to 325°F (165°C). In a bowl, sift together the flour and ½ cup (4 oz/125 g) of the sugar. Repeat the sifting 3 more times.

In the bowl of a stand mixer fitted with the whisk attachment, beat the egg whites on low speed until they begin to foam, about 2 minutes. Add the salt, cream of tartar, and vanilla, raise the speed to medium, and beat until soft peaks form, about 4 minutes. With the mixer running, slowly add the remaining 1 cup (8 oz/250 g) sugar. Raise the speed to high and beat until stiff peaks form, about 2 minutes. Remove the bowl from the mixer and sprinkle the flour mixture over the egg white mixture. Using a rubber spatula, gently fold in the flour mixture, taking care not to overmix.

Spoon the batter into an ungreased angel food cake pan, then gently tap the pan on the counter to release any air pockets. Bake until the cake is golden brown and springs back when lightly touched, 35–45 minutes. Invert the pan onto a wire rack and let cool upside down for about 30 minutes. To release, run a paring knife around the edges of the pan. Turn right side up on the rack and let cool for 10 minutes longer.

Meanwhile, make the minted strawberries: In a large bowl, stir together the strawberries, sugar, and chopped mint. Let stand until the juices have released, about 25 minutes. Make the mascarpone whipped cream. Top the cake with the mascarpone whipped cream, minted strawberries, and whole mint leaves, and serve.

TIP *For a beautifully tiered angel food cake, carefully cut the cake horizontally into three layers, topping each one with whipped cream and strawberries.*

DREAMY FILLING

The mix of smooth mascarpone and fluffy whipped cream creates the ideal balance between rich and light.

SPARKLE & SHINE
Candied blood oranges
take center stage atop
vanilla-bean studded
buttercream frosting.

Light and airy, chiffon cakes rely on whipped egg whites to help them rise. Unlike angel food cake, chiffon also contains fat in the form of egg yolks and oil to keep it moist. Orange zest adds the perfume of citrus, and sweet-tart candied blood oranges add beauty and delicious sophistication.

BLOOD ORANGE CHIFFON CAKE

1 recipe Candied Blood Oranges (page 105)

FOR THE CAKE

½ cup (125 ml) canola oil, plus more for greasing

2 cups (10 oz/315 g) all-purpose flour, sifted, plus more for dusting

1½ cups (12 oz/375 g) sugar

2 tablespoons grated orange zest

1 tablespoon baking powder

1 teaspoon kosher salt

6 large eggs, separated

½ teaspoon cream of tartar

¾ cup (180 ml) whole milk

1 teaspoon pure vanilla extract

1 tablespoon orange blossom water (optional)

2 recipes Traditional Vanilla Buttercream (page 97)

1 vanilla bean, split and seeds scraped, seeds reserved

Serves 12

Make the candied blood oranges as directed. Set aside.

Preheat the oven to 325°F (165°C). Grease two 9-inch (23-cm) round cake pans, line the bottoms with parchment paper, then grease the parchment. Dust with flour, then tap out any excess.

Place 1 cup (8 oz/250 g) of the sugar in a bowl. Using your fingers, rub the orange zest into the sugar to release the oils. Whisk in the flour, baking powder, and salt. Set aside. In the bowl of a stand mixer fitted with the whisk attachment, beat the egg whites on medium speed until foamy, about 30 seconds. Add the cream of tartar and the remaining ½ cup (4 oz/125 g) sugar, raise the speed to medium-high, and beat until stiff peaks form, about 3 minutes. Set aside.

In the clean bowl of the stand mixer fitted with the clean whisk attachment, beat together the egg yolks, oil, milk, vanilla, and orange blossom water (if using) on medium speed until pale yellow, about 2 minutes. Stop the mixer, add the flour mixture, and beat on low speed until combined, about 30 seconds. Stop the mixer and scrape down the sides of the bowl, then beat on high speed for 30 seconds. Using a rubber spatula, gently fold in the egg whites until just combined, taking care not to deflate the peaks.

Continued on page 42

Continued from page 41

BLOOD ORANGE CHIFFON CAKE

Divide the batter evenly between the prepared pans. Bake until a toothpick inserted into the center of the cakes comes out clean, about 40 minutes. Let the cakes cool in the pans on wire racks for 10 minutes, then invert the cakes onto the racks and let cool completely.

Make the traditional vanilla buttercream, adding the vanilla bean seeds along with the extract.

To assemble the cake, place 1 cake layer on a serving plate. Spread an even layer of buttercream over the cake, then top with the other cake layer. Refrigerate until set, about 10 minutes. Frost the outside of the cake as desired with the remaining buttercream. Arrange the candied blood orange slices on top of the cake and around the base and serve.

TIP *If blood oranges aren't in season, use any citrus instead.*

Pineapple upside-down cake never goes out of fashion—it's a classic, and for good reason. The sweet tang of caramelized pineapple is an exquisite partner to the tender, brown butter–rich cake.

BROWN BUTTER PINEAPPLE UPSIDE-DOWN CAKE

½ cup (4 oz/125 g) unsalted butter, plus more for greasing

1½ cups (7½ oz/235 g) all-purpose flour, plus more for dusting

1 teaspoon baking powder

½ teaspoon *each* baking soda and kosher salt

1 cup (8 oz/250 g) granulated sugar

1 large egg plus 1 large egg yolk

1½ teaspoons pure vanilla extract

1 cup (250 ml) buttermilk

2 tablespoons unsalted butter, melted and cooled

2 tablespoons firmly packed light brown sugar

1 can (20 oz/567 g) sliced pineapple, drained

1 recipe Brown Butter Glaze (page 104)

Serves 10–12

In a large sauté pan over medium heat, melt the butter. Reduce the heat to medium-low and simmer gently, swirling the pan often, until the butter is toasty brown and smells nutty, 5–7 minutes. Watch carefully at the end to prevent the butter from burning. Transfer to a bowl and let cool to room temperature, then refrigerate the brown butter until it is the consistency of softened butter, 30–60 minutes.

Preheat the oven to 350°F (180°C). Grease a 9-inch (23-cm) springform pan, line the bottom of the pan with parchment paper, then grease the parchment. Dust with flour, then tap out any excess.

In a bowl, sift together the flour, baking powder, baking soda, and salt. Set aside. In the bowl of a stand mixer fitted with the paddle attachment, beat together the brown butter and granulated sugar on medium speed until light and fluffy, about 2 minutes. Add the egg, egg yolk, and vanilla and beat until combined. Stop the mixer and scrape down the sides of the bowl. With the mixer on low speed, add the flour mixture in 3 additions, alternating with the buttermilk and beginning and ending with the flour, and beat until combined. Stop the mixer and scrape down the sides of the bowl. Raise the speed to high and beat for 30 seconds.

In a small bowl, stir together the melted butter and brown sugar. Spread evenly in the prepared pan. Arrange the pineapple slices on top, slightly overlapping them. Pour the batter on top and spread evenly. Bake until a toothpick inserted into the center comes out clean, about 45 minutes. Let cool in the pan on a wire rack for 10 minutes, then remove the pan's outer ring and invert the cake onto a platter.

Make the glaze as directed and pour over the warm cake. Serve warm or at room temperature.

SWIRLS OF BEAUTY
The meringue florets that adorn this naturally leavened cake are created using an open star piping tip.

This swoon-worthy dessert is a riff on lemon meringue pie, featuring three lemony cake layers spread with lemon curd and fluffy meringue frosting. Use a kitchen torch to easily toast the meringue to a golden brown hue.

LEMON GENOISE CAKE WITH MERINGUE FROSTING

1 recipe Lemon Curd
(page 90)

½ cup (2½ oz/75 g)
all-purpose flour

½ cup (2 oz/60 g) cornstarch

9 large eggs, separated,
plus 1 large egg

1 cup (8 oz/250 g) sugar

1½ tablespoons grated
lemon zest

¾ cup (6 oz/185 g) unsalted
butter, melted and cooled

1 recipe Meringue Frosting
(page 101)

Serves 12

Make the lemon curd and refrigerate as directed.

Preheat the oven to 325°F (165°C). In a bowl, sift together the flour and cornstarch. Set aside.

In the bowl of a stand mixer fitted with the whisk attachment, beat together the egg yolks and egg on medium speed until combined. Raise the speed to medium-high, slowly add ½ cup (4 oz/125 g) of the sugar, and beat until the mixture is pale and has tripled in volume, 3–5 minutes. Transfer the egg yolk mixture to a bowl and set aside.

In the clean bowl of the stand mixer fitted with the clean whisk attachment, beat the egg whites on medium speed until foamy. Raise the speed to medium-high, slowly add the remaining ½ cup (4 oz/125 g) sugar, and beat until stiff peaks form, 3–5 minutes. Remove the bowl from the mixer and, using a rubber spatula, carefully fold the egg yolk mixture into the egg white mixture. (This is the opposite of the usual technique, but it's correct.) Add the lemon zest. Sift the flour mixture over the egg mixture and fold until the flour streaks begin to disappear. Add the melted butter and fold until just combined.

Continued on page 46

Continued from page 45

LEMON GENOISE CAKE
WITH MERINGUE FROSTING

Divide the batter evenly among three ungreased 8-inch (20-cm) round cake pans and spread evenly. Bake until the cakes spring back when lightly touched and a toothpick inserted into the center comes out with just a few moist crumbs attached, about 30 minutes. Transfer the pans to wire racks, let cool for 10 minutes, then invert the cakes onto the rack and let cool completely.

To assemble the cake, place 1 cake layer on a cake stand. Spread half of the lemon curd over the cake. Top with a second cake layer and spread the remaining lemon curd over the cake. Top with the third cake layer and refrigerate while you prepare the meringue.

Make the meringue frosting: Fill a large pastry bag fitted with an open star tip with the meringue, being careful not to deflate the meringue. Starting at the bottom of the cake, pipe florets along and up the sides, finishing on the top. Using a kitchen torch, toast the meringue until nicely browned.

TIP   *If you don't have three cake pans, divide the batter between two 9-inch (23-cm) cake pans and make a two-layer cake. Keep in mind that this batter will deflate if not used right away.*

When baked, this flourless dark chocolate cake puffs up almost like a soufflé, then gently falls and cracks as it cools, leaving a delightfully crisp crust and a tender, rich interior. It also leaves a hollow in the center of the cake, perfect for filling with Frangelico-scented whipped cream, toasty chopped hazelnuts, and pretty chocolate shavings.

FLOURLESS CHOCOLATE & HAZELNUT FALLEN CAKE

½ cup (4 oz/125 g) unsalted butter, cut into cubes, plus more for greasing

¾ cup (6 oz/185 g) granulated sugar, plus more for dusting

10 oz (315 g) semisweet chocolate, chopped

2 tablespoons canola oil

4 large eggs, separated, plus 2 large eggs

2 tablespoons Frangelico

2 tablespoons unsweetened cocoa powder

1 teaspoon pure vanilla extract

1 teaspoon kosher salt

¾ cup (2¾ oz/75 g) finely ground hazelnuts

1 recipe Frangelico Whipped Cream (page 91)

Chopped toasted hazelnuts, for garnish

Shaved chocolate, for garnish

Serves 8–10

Preheat the oven to 350°F (180°C). Grease a 9-inch (23-cm) springform pan, line the bottom of the pan with parchment paper, then grease the parchment. Dust with granulated sugar, then tap out any excess.

Combine the butter, chocolate, and oil in a large heatproof bowl and set over but not touching barely simmering water in a saucepan. Heat, stirring occasionally, until melted and smooth, about 4 minutes. Remove the bowl from the heat.

In the bowl of a stand mixer fitted with the whisk attachment, beat the egg whites on medium-high speed until frothy, about 1 minute. Add ½ cup (4 oz/125 g) of the granulated sugar and beat until stiff peaks form, about 3 minutes. Set aside.

In a medium bowl, whisk together the egg yolks, eggs, Frangelico, the remaining ¼ cup (2 oz/60 g) granulated sugar, cocoa powder, vanilla, and salt until smooth. Add the egg yolk mixture to the chocolate mixture and whisk until incorporated, about 1 minute. Fold one-fourth of the egg whites and all of the ground hazelnuts into the chocolate mixture, then gently fold in the remaining egg whites until uniformly combined.

Pour the batter into the prepared pan and spread evenly. Bake until the cake has risen above the rim of the pan and is set on top, 35–40 minutes. Transfer the pan to a wire rack and let cool completely. The cake will fall slightly and crack on top as it cools.

Make the Frangelico whipped cream: Remove the outer ring of the pan. Mound the whipped cream in the center of the cake and garnish with chopped hazelnuts and shaved chocolate.

By layering lots of thin, eggy crepes with dulce de leche–flavored whipped cream, then topping the whole thing off with dulce de leche sauce, you end up with a gorgeous dessert fit for the most decadent of fêtes. Double the recipe for a magnificently tall cake.

DULCE DE LECHE CREPE CAKE

FOR THE CREPES

9 large eggs

1½ cups (12 oz/375 ml) whole milk

1½ cups (7½ oz/235 g) all-purpose flour

¼ cup (1 oz/30 g) plus 1 tablespoon confectioners' sugar

1 tablespoon pure vanilla extract

1½ teaspoons kosher salt

FOR THE DULCE DE LECHE WHIPPED CREAM

1 cup (8 oz/250 g) plus 2 tablespoons granulated sugar

6 tablespoons (3 oz/90 g) cold unsalted butter, cut into small pieces

1 teaspoon kosher salt

1½ cups (12 oz/375 ml) evaporated milk

3 cups (24 oz/750 ml) heavy cream

Serves 8–10

To make the crepes, in a blender, combine the eggs, milk, flour, confectioners' sugar, vanilla, and salt and blend until well combined, about 45 seconds. Stop the blender and scrape down the sides of the bowl, then blend for 30 seconds longer.

Line a baking sheet with parchment paper. Heat a 10-inch (25-cm) crepe pan or nonstick frying pan over medium-low heat (do not grease the pan). Ladle about ¼ cup (60 ml) of the batter into the center of the pan, then quickly lift and rotate the pan to spread the batter to the edges. If the batter begins to set before spreading, reduce the heat. Cook until the crepe is almost completely cooked through, about 2 minutes. Using a rubber spatula and your fingers, carefully flip the crepe over and cook for 15 seconds longer. Transfer the crepe to the prepared baking sheet to cool. Repeat with the remaining batter, stacking the crepes on top of each other. Let the crepes cool completely before assembling the cake.

Continued on page 50

IN BLOOM
A last-minute sprinkling
of edible spring blooms add
a touch of elegance to this
creative crepe confection.

Continued from page 48

DULCE DE LECHE CREPE CAKE

To make the dulce de leche, prepare an ice water bath in a large bowl. Put the granulated sugar in a large saucepan, place over medium-high heat, and stir until the sugar begins to melt. Continue stirring, breaking up clumps of sugar as they form, until all of the sugar has melted and turned a golden caramel color, 8–10 minutes. Add the butter (the mixture will start to bubble) and stir until the butter has melted. While stirring constantly, slowly stir in the evaporated milk (the mixture will continue to bubble) and cook, stirring occasionally, until the mixture is bubbling toward the top of the pan and has formed a cohesive caramel-like texture, about 5 minutes. Place the saucepan in the ice bath and stir until the sauce is cool to the touch, then let stand at room temperature to cool completely.

In the bowl of a stand mixer fitted with the whisk attachment, beat the cream on medium-high speed until soft peaks form, about 3 minutes. Remove the bowl from the mixer. Using a rubber spatula, fold in about half of the dulce de leche until fully incorporated. Reserve the remaining dulce de leche for drizzling over the cake.

To assemble the cake, place 1 crepe on a cake stand or serving plate. Top with a generous dollop of the dulce de leche whipped cream and spread evenly over the crepe. Repeat with the remaining crepes and whipped cream. Refrigerate until ready to serve.

Just before serving, heat the remaining dulce de leche over low heat until slightly loosened but not hot. Pour over the cake and let drizzle down the sides. The cake can be stored in an airtight container at room temperature for up to 2 days.

TIP   *For a 40-layer cake, double the recipe by making the crepe batter in two additions. Double the dulce de leche whipped cream recipe and assemble as directed.*

Rich with pungent extra-virgin olive oil, this tender cake is a natural partner to lightly sweetened cherry compote. Use fresh cherries at the peak of their season, and choose frozen cherries other times of the year. A dollop of lightly whipped cream is the natural accompaniment.

CHERRY-OLIVE OIL CAKE

FOR THE CAKE

1 cup (250 ml) extra-virgin olive oil, plus more for greasing

2 cups (10 oz/315 g) all-purpose flour, sifted

1 cup (8 oz/250 g) granulated sugar

1 cup (7 oz/220 g) firmly packed light brown sugar

1 teaspoon baking powder

1 teaspoon kosher salt

1 cup (250 ml) whole milk

3 large eggs

Zest of 1 lemon

1½ cups (9 oz/280 g) pitted fresh or thawed frozen cherries

FOR THE CHERRY COMPOTE

1½ cups (9 oz/280 g) pitted fresh or thawed frozen cherries

½ cup (3½ oz/105 g) firmly packed light brown sugar

Juice of 1 lemon

Confectioners' sugar, for dusting

Serves 12

To make the cake, preheat the oven to 350°F (180°C). Grease a 9-inch (23-cm) round cake pan, line the bottom of the pan with parchment paper, then grease the parchment.

In a medium bowl, whisk together the flour, both sugars, baking powder, and salt. In a large bowl, whisk together the oil, milk, eggs, and lemon zest, then stir in the flour mixture until combined. Using a rubber spatula, fold in the cherries.

Pour the batter into the prepared pan and spread evenly. Bake until a toothpick inserted into the center of the cake comes out clean, about 1 hour. Transfer the pan to a wire rack and let cool for 10 minutes, then invert the cake onto the rack and let cool completely.

Meanwhile, make the cherry compote: In a saucepan over medium heat, combine the cherries, brown sugar, and lemon juice and bring to a simmer. Cook, stirring occasionally, until thickened, about 10 minutes. Let cool to room temperature before serving. The compote can be stored in an airtight container in the refrigerator for up to 1 week.

Just before serving, dust the cake with confectioners' sugar and top with the cherry compote.

FANCY FINISH
Embellish the cake with
a liberal sprinkling of lightly
toasted sliced almonds.

Pears poached in amaretto are a tasty dessert in their own right, but serve slices of the sweet poached fruit atop dark chocolate cake layered with mascarpone whipped cream and the result is truly magnificent.

CHOCOLATE ALMOND CAKE WITH POACHED PEARS

1 recipe Amaretto-Poached Pears (page 104)

1 recipe Almond-Mascarpone Whipped Cream (page 91)

FOR THE CAKE

¾ cup (6 oz/185 g) unsalted butter, at room temperature, plus more for greasing

2 cups (10 oz/315 g) all-purpose flour, plus more for dusting

6 oz (185 g) semisweet chocolate

½ cup (125 ml) whole milk

¾ cup (6 oz/185 g) *each* granulated sugar and firmly packed light brown sugar

3 tablespoons unsweetened cocoa powder

2 teaspoons baking powder

¾ teaspoon kosher salt

3 large eggs

1 teaspoon pure vanilla extract

⅓ cup (2½ oz/75 g) sour cream

Serves 12

Make the amaretto-poached pears and almond-mascarpone whipped cream as directed. Cover and refrigerate until ready to use.

To make the cake, preheat the oven to 325°F (165°C). Grease two 8-inch (20-cm) round cake pans, line the bottoms of the pans with parchment paper, then grease the parchment. Dust with flour, then tap out any excess.

Combine the butter, chocolate, and milk in a heatproof bowl and set over but not touching barely simmering water in a saucepan. Heat, stirring occasionally, until melted, about 8 minutes. Remove from the heat and whisk to combine. Set aside.

In a large bowl, sift together the flour, both sugars, cocoa powder, baking powder, and salt. Whisk in the eggs and vanilla. Whisk the sour cream into the chocolate mixture, then add to the flour mixture and whisk until completely incorporated. Divide the batter evenly among the prepared pans. Bake until a toothpick inserted into the center of the cakes comes out clean, 35–40 minutes. Transfer the pans to wire racks and let cool for 10 minutes, then invert the cakes onto the racks and let cool completely.

To assemble the cake, place 1 cake layer on a cake stand or serving plate. Spread half of the almond-mascarpone whipped cream evenly over the cake, then top with the other cake layer. Spread the remaining whipped cream, except for ¼ cup (60 ml), evenly over the cake. Using an offset spatula, spread the reserved whipped cream in a very thin layer on the sides to create a "naked" cake effect. Refrigerate until set, about 20 minutes.

Arrange the pears on top of the cake. If desired, pour the poaching liquid through a fine-mesh sieve and drizzle over the top. Serve.

SPECIALTY CAKES

EASY DOES IT
Use food coloring sparingly,
mixing well before adding
more until you achieve
the color you desire.

Ombré is the gradual blending of one shade to another, and in this gorgeous layer cake, we chose pink-berry hues to construct a party-worthy dessert. You'll need four cake pans for this tall cake, as each layer must be baked separately to create the multi-colored effect. Once layered, the cake is covered in easy-to-pipe rosettes.

VANILLA OMBRÉ LAYER CAKE

FOR THE CAKE

Unsalted butter, for greasing

All-purpose flour, for dusting

1 recipe White Cake (page 92)

Pink, red, or other food coloring of choice

FOR THE BUTTERCREAM

5 cups (2½ lb/1.25 kg) unsalted butter, at room temperature

8 cups (2 lb/1 kg) confectioners' sugar

5 teaspoons pure vanilla extract

½ teaspoon kosher salt

Serves 12

To make the cake, place 1 rack in the upper third and 1 rack in the lower third of the oven and preheat to 350°F (180°C). Grease four 8-inch (20-cm) round cake pans, line the bottoms of the pans with parchment paper, then grease the parchment. Dust with flour, then tap out any excess.

Make the white cake batter and divide it evenly among 4 bowls. Add food coloring to 3 of the bowls, making light, medium, and dark shades of the same color. Stir the batter until the food coloring is completely blended. Leave 1 bowl of batter plain.

Pour each batter into a prepared pan and spread evenly. Bake, rotating the pans between the racks halfway through baking, until a toothpick inserted into the center of the cakes comes out clean, 15–20 minutes. Transfer the pans to wire racks and let cool for 10 minutes, then invert the cakes onto the racks and let cool completely.

To make the buttercream, in the bowl of a stand mixer fitted with the paddle attachment, beat the butter on medium speed until smooth, about 3 minutes. Add the confectioners' sugar in 3 additions, beating well after each one. Add the vanilla and salt, raise the speed to medium-high, and beat until combined, stopping the mixer to scrape down the sides of the bowl as needed.

Continued on page 58

Continued from page 57

VANILLA OMBRÉ LAYER CAKE

Reserve half of the plain buttercream for the filling, crumb coat, and bottom layer of frosting. Spoon half of the remaining buttercream into a bowl, then add food coloring to make it the darkest shade. Divide the remaining buttercream among 2 bowls and add food coloring to to make light and medium shades. Stir the buttercream until the food coloring is completely blended.

To assemble the cake, place the plain cake layer on a cake stand or serving plate. Spread about ¼ cup (60 ml) of the plain buttercream evenly over the cake, then top with the lightest dyed cake layer. Repeat with the remaining cake layers, ending with the darkest one. Spread a very thin layer of plain buttercream over the top and sides of the cake. Refrigerate until you are ready to pipe the rosettes.

Transfer the remaining plain buttercream to a large pastry bag fitted with a large closed star tip. Starting at the bottom of the cake, pipe a single row of rosettes. Repeat with the lightest-colored buttercream (using a clean pastry bag and tip), followed by the medium buttercream, then pipe the darkest shade in a single row of rosettes on the side of the cake and all over the top of the cake and serve.

This sweet, impressive cake—which hails from Russia—has eight delicate, honey-infused layers that are made from a cookie-like dough. Once rolled, cut, and baked, the layers are sandwiched with a mixture of whipped cream and sour cream, which softens them to a melt-in-your-mouth texture. A dusting of pistachios adds both color and texture to the top of the cake.

8-LAYER HONEY-PISTACHIO CAKE

FOR THE CAKE

3 cups (15 oz/470 g) all-purpose flour, plus more for dusting

1 teaspoon baking soda

¼ teaspoon kosher salt

½ cup (6 oz/185 g) honey

½ cup (4 oz/125 g) granulated sugar

2 tablespoons unsalted butter

3 large eggs

FOR THE SOUR CREAM FROSTING

1 cup (250 ml) heavy cream

4 cups (2 lb/1 kg) sour cream

2 cups (8 oz/250 g) confectioners' sugar

1 teaspoon pure vanilla extract

¼ teaspoon kosher salt

½ cup (2 oz/60 g) toasted pistachios, crushed

Serves 12

To make the cake, preheat the oven to 350°F (180°C). Line a baking sheet with parchment paper.

In a bowl, sift together the flour, baking soda, and salt. Set aside. In a large saucepan over medium heat, combine the honey, granulated sugar, and butter and cook, stirring occasionally, until the butter melts and the sugar and honey dissolve, about 5 minutes. Remove from the heat and let cool slightly.

In a small bowl, whisk the eggs until blended. Add a small amount of the honey mixture to the eggs and whisk to combine. While whisking constantly, gradually add the egg mixture to the honey mixture in the saucepan. Using a rubber spatula, fold in the flour mixture until almost incorporated, then transfer to a lightly floured surface and knead just to form a disk. Divide the disk into 8 equal pieces.

Roll out each piece of dough into a 9-inch (23-cm) round. Using an 8-inch (20-cm) plate or cake pan for tracing, cut each piece into an 8-inch (20-cm) round, reserving the scraps. Transfer 2 rounds to the prepared baking sheet and bake until crisp and golden brown, about 6 minutes. Transfer to a wire rack and let cool. Repeat with the remaining rounds. The cooled rounds should have the texture of graham crackers. Place the reserved dough scraps in a single layer on the baking sheet and bake until crisp and golden brown, about 6 minutes. Set aside.

Continued on page 60

Continued from page 59

8-LAYER HONEY-PISTACHIO CAKE

To make the sour cream frosting, in the bowl of a stand mixer fitted with the whisk attachment, beat the cream on medium-high speed until stiff peaks form, about 3 minutes. In a large bowl, using a handheld whisk, whisk together the sour cream, confectioners' sugar, vanilla, and salt. Using a rubber spatula, fold in the whipped cream.

To assemble the cake, place 1 cake round on a parchment-lined baking sheet or a cake circle. Spread about ½ cup (125 ml) of the sour cream frosting evenly over the disk, all the way to the edges (it's okay if some spills over). Top with another cake round and spread with frosting, then repeat with the remaining cake rounds. Spread the remaining frosting evenly over the top and sides of the cake. Using a small food processor, or a plastic bag and a rolling pin, crush the scrap pieces. Press the crumbs onto the sides of the cake. Sprinkle the pistachios over the top.

Refrigerate the cake overnight; the frosting will soften the layers into a cakelike texture. Serve chilled or at room temperature.

TIP *This cake is a lovely balance of rich honey and tart sour cream. To make it sweeter, add an additional 1 cup (4 oz/125 g) confectioners' sugar to the frosting.*

FLOWER POWER
You can substitute lavender
extract for dried lavender;
add 1 drop at a time to the
batter, tasting as you go.

This moist layered pound cake makes the perfect finale to a summer barbecue. To tint the vanilla buttercream a pretty shade of pale purple, stir in a little fresh blackberry juice—made by pressing a handful of blackberries through a fine-mesh sieve.

LAVENDER-BLACKBERRY POUND CAKE

FOR THE CAKE

1½ cups (¾ lb/375 g) unsalted butter, at room temperature, plus more for greasing

3 cups (15 oz/470 g) all-purpose flour, plus more for dusting

1½ teaspoons baking powder

¾ teaspoon kosher salt

2¼ cups (18 oz/560 g) sugar

1 teaspoon dried lavender, very finely minced

4 large eggs plus 1 large egg white

3 teaspoons pure vanilla extract

1 cup (250 ml) whole milk

5 pints (2½ lb/1.25 kg) blackberries

½ recipe Traditional Vanilla Buttercream (page 97)

1 tablespoon sugar

Fresh lavender or other edible flowers, for decorating

Serves 12

Preheat the oven to 350°F (180°C). Grease two 8-inch (20-cm) round cake pans, line the bottoms of the pans with parchment paper, then grease the parchment. Dust with flour, then tap out any excess.

In a large bowl, sift together the flour, baking powder, and salt. Set aside. In a food processor, combine the butter, sugar, and dried lavender and pulse until well combined, about 45 seconds. Transfer the butter mixture to the bowl of a stand mixer fitted with the paddle attachment. On medium speed, beat in the eggs and egg white one at a time, beating well after each addition, then beat in the vanilla. Reduce the speed to low and add the flour mixture in 3 additions, alternating with the milk and beginning and ending with the flour, and beat until combined.

Arrange a single layer of blackberries on the bottom of the prepared pans so that they cover the entire surface (about 2 pints/1 lb/500 g per pan); reserve the remaining berries for decorating. Divide the batter evenly between the pans and spread evenly. Tap the pans on the counter to submerge the berries in the batter. Bake until a toothpick inserted into the center of the cakes comes out clean, about 50 minutes. Transfer the pans to wire racks and let cool for 10 minutes, then invert the cakes onto the racks and let cool completely.

Make the traditional vanilla buttercream. To assemble the cake, place 1 cake layer, blackberry side up, on a serving plate. Spread half of the buttercream evenly over the cake, then top with the other layer, blackberry side up. Spread the remaining buttercream over the top of the cake. In a small bowl, toss together the remaining blackberries and the sugar until evenly coated. Arrange them in a ring around the outside edge of the cake, decorate with fresh lavender, and serve.

This is the ultimate ice cream cake: layers of chocolate cake are filled with rich chocolate ganache and homemade strawberry and vanilla "ice cream." Once frozen, the cake is frosted with fluffy whipped cream, then topped with more of the ganache. An ice cream cone covered in sprinkles makes for a playful and easy decoration to top it all off.

NEAPOLITAN "ICE CREAM" CAKE

FOR THE CHOCOLATE CAKE

¼ cup (60 ml) canola oil, plus more for greasing

1¼ cups (6½ oz/200 g) all-purpose flour

½ cup (1½ oz/45 g) unsweetened cocoa powder

¾ teaspoon baking powder

¾ teaspoon baking soda

¾ teaspoon kosher salt

1 cup (8 oz/250 g) granulated sugar

1 large egg plus 1 large egg yolk

¾ cup (180 ml) buttermilk

2 teaspoons pure vanilla extract

3 oz (90 g) semisweet chocolate chips, melted and cooled

½ teaspoon espresso powder

FOR THE GANACHE FILLING AND TOPPING

1½ cups (360 ml) heavy cream

11 oz (340 g) dark chocolate

To make the cake, preheat the oven to 350°F (180°C). Grease a 9-inch (23-cm) springform pan, line the bottom of the pan with parchment paper, then grease the parchment.

In a bowl, sift together the flour, cocoa powder, baking powder, baking soda, and salt. Set aside.

In the bowl of a stand mixer fitted with the paddle attachment, beat together the granulated sugar, egg, egg yolk, buttermilk, oil, and vanilla on medium speed until combined, about 2 minutes. Reduce the speed to low, slowly add the flour mixture, and beat until combined, stopping the mixer to scrape down the sides of the bowl as needed. Add the melted chocolate and espresso powder and beat until combined. Raise the speed to high and beat for 20 seconds.

Pour the batter into the prepared pan and spread evenly. Bake until a toothpick inserted into the center of the cake comes out clean, 28–30 minutes. Transfer the pan to a wire rack and let cool completely. Remove the outer ring of the springform pan and set aside.

To make the ganache filling, in a small saucepan over medium-high heat, bring ¾ cup (180 ml) of the cream to a boil. Place 5 oz (155 g) of the chocolate in a heatproof bowl and pour the hot cream over the chocolate. Let stand for 5 minutes, then whisk to combine. Let cool completely.

To make the strawberry layer, in the clean bowl of the stand mixer fitted with the clean paddle attachment, beat together the cream cheese and granulated sugar on medium-high speed until combined. Add the milk and food coloring and beat for 30 seconds. Transfer the mixture to a large bowl and wash and dry the mixer bowl.

Continued on page 66

SWEET SWAP
You can replace the
strawberry and vanilla
ice cream with any
of your favorite flavors.

Continued from page 64

NEAPOLITAN "ICE CREAM" CAKE

FOR THE STRAWBERRY LAYER

½ lb (250 g) cream cheese, at room temperature

½ cup (4 oz/125 g) plus 1 tablespoon granulated sugar

2 tablespoons whole milk

1 drop red food coloring

1 cup (250 ml) heavy cream

1 cup (1 oz/25 g) freeze-dried strawberries

FOR THE VANILLA LAYER

½ lb (250 g) cream cheese, at room temperature

½ cup (4 oz/125 g) plus 1 tablespoon granulated sugar

2 tablespoons whole milk

1 teaspoon pure vanilla extract

1 vanilla bean, split and seeds scraped, seeds reserved

1 cup (250 ml) heavy cream

FOR THE WHIPPED CREAM ICING

1½ cups (375 ml) heavy cream

¾ cup (3 oz/95 g) confectioners' sugar

½ teaspoon pure vanilla extract

FOR DECORATING

1 scoop vanilla ice cream

1 ice cream cone

Rainbow sprinkles

Serves 16–20

Pour the cream into the mixer bowl, fit the mixer with the whisk attachment, and beat on medium-high speed until medium to stiff peaks form. Using a rubber spatula, fold the whipped cream into the cream cheese mixture, then fold in the strawberries. Set aside.

To make the vanilla layer, in the clean bowl of the stand mixer fitted with the clean paddle attachment, beat together the cream cheese and granulated sugar on medium-high speed until combined. Add the milk, vanilla extract, and vanilla bean seeds and beat for 30 seconds. Transfer the mixture to a large bowl and wash and dry the mixer bowl. Pour the cream into the mixer bowl, fit the mixer with the clean whisk attachment, and beat on medium-high speed until medium to stiff peaks form. Using a rubber spatula, fold the whipped cream into the cream cheese mixture. Set aside.

To assemble the cake, line the sides of the springform pan with parchment paper so that the parchment extends about 4 inches (10 cm) above the top of the pan. Using a large serrated knife, cut the cake in half horizontally. Place one half in the pan. Spread half of the ganache evenly over the cake, then spread the strawberry filling over the top. Place the second half of the cake and spread with the remaining ganache, then spread the vanilla filling evenly on top. Freeze for at least 6 hours or up to overnight.

Remove the cake from the pan and remove the parchment. Place the cake on a cake stand or serving plate.

To make the whipped cream icing, in the clean bowl of the stand mixer fitted with the clean whisk attachment, beat together the cream, confectioners' sugar, and vanilla on medium-high speed until stiff peaks form, about 3 minutes. Spread the whipped cream over the the cake. Freeze until ready to serve, at least 1 hour or up to 3 days.

Just before serving, make the ganache topping: In a small saucepan over medium-high heat, bring the remaining ¾ cup (180 ml) cream to a boil. Place the remaining 6 oz (185 g) chocolate in a heatproof bowl and pour the hot cream over the chocolate. Let stand for 5 minutes, then whisk to combine. Let cool slightly. Remove the cake from the freezer and pour the ganache over the top, allowing some of it to drip over the sides. This will happen quickly since the cake is frozen. Scoop vanilla ice cream into the cone and cover with sprinkles. Place it upside down on top of the cake, holding it for a few seconds until it stays. Decorate the top of the cake with sprinkles. The cake can be wrapped in plastic wrap and stored in the freezer for up to 1 week.

Flavored with orange zest, vanilla bean, and orange blossom water, this moist, tender cake has enough fragrant flavor to stand on its own, but add a dollop of whipped cream and a smattering of blackberries to individual portions before serving, if you like. Seek out a good-quality gluten-free flour mix, like Cup4Cup.

GLUTEN-FREE ALMOND & ORANGE BLOSSOM CAKE

Butter for greasing

1 cup (5 oz/140 g) gluten-free flour, plus more for dusting

1 cup (3 oz/90 g) almond meal

1 teaspoon baking powder

½ teaspoon kosher salt

4 large eggs, separated

1½ cups (12 oz/375 g) granulated sugar

Zest of 1 orange

1 tablespoon orange blossom water

1 teaspoon pure vanilla extract

½ teaspoon almond extract

1 vanilla bean, split and seeds scraped, seeds reserved

Confectioners' sugar, for dusting

Serves 12

Preheat the oven to 350°F (180°C). Grease a 9-inch (23-cm) springform pan, line the bottom of the pan with parchment paper, then grease the parchment. Lightly dust the pan with gluten-free flour or confectioners' sugar, then tap out any excess.

In a bowl, whisk together the gluten-free flour, almond meal, baking powder, and salt. Set aside.

In the bowl of a stand mixer fitted with the whisk attachment, beat together the egg yolks and 1 cup (8 oz/250 g) of the sugar on medium speed until pale yellow and thick, about 3 minutes. Stop the mixer and add the orange zest, orange blossom water, vanilla and almond extracts, and vanilla bean seeds. Beat on medium-high speed until combined, about 1 minute. Transfer to a large bowl and set aside.

In the clean bowl of the stand mixer fitted with the clean whisk attachment, beat the egg whites on medium-high speed until soft peaks form, about 3 minutes. With the mixer running, slowly add the remaining ½ cup (4 oz/125 g) sugar and beat until stiff peaks form, about 2 minutes.

Using a rubber spatula, fold half of the flour mixture into the yolk mixture until combined, then gently fold in half of the egg white mixture until combined, taking care not to deflate the peaks. Fold in the remaining flour and then the remaining egg whites.

Transfer the batter to the prepared pan. Bake until a toothpick inserted into the center of the cake comes out clean, about 45 minutes. Transfer the pan to a wire rack and let cool slightly for 10 minutes, then run an offset spatula around the edges and remove the outer ring of the pan. Dust the cake with confectioners' sugar and serve warm or at room temperature.

CHANGE IT UP
To decorate this cake
as a dog or cat, simply
make adjustments to the
colors and the ears, nose,
and cheek shapes.

This sweet chocolate layer cake, decorated as a fox, is about as cute as they come. The result is so impressive that everyone will think the cake came straight from a bakery. But read through these easy steps—you'll see that it's much easier to make than it looks!

FOX CHOCOLATE LAYER CAKE

1 recipe Chocolate Cake (page 95)

2 recipes Quick Vanilla Buttercream (page 97)

Black, red, and yellow food coloring

Serves 12

Make the chocolate cake batter, bake as directed in two 8-inch (20-cm) round cake pans, and let cool completely. Make the quick vanilla buttercream.

To assemble the cake, place 1 cake layer on a cake stand or serving plate. Spread about 1 cup (250 ml) of the buttercream evenly over the cake, then top with the other layer. Refrigerate until set, about 20 minutes.

Transfer ½ cup (125 ml) of the buttercream to a pastry bag fitted with a small round tip. Place 1 cup (250 ml) of the buttercream in a small bowl and add black food coloring until a dark shade is reached. Transfer to another pastry bag fitted with a small round tip.

Add red and yellow food coloring to the remaining buttercream until the desired reddish-orange shade is reached (the color of a fox). Transfer to a third pastry bag fitted with a large star or multi-opening tip. Starting on the sides of the cake, pipe reddish-orange fox "fur," covering the sides completely. Then pipe "fur" over the top of the cake, leaving 2 oval-shaped pockets empty for the fox "cheeks." Pipe the remaining reddish-orange buttercream in 2 pyramid shapes to form the ears (place toothpicks behind the ears to support them).

Using the plain buttercream, fill in the cheeks. Using the black buttercream, fill in the inner ears and add a nose, eyes, and eyebrows. Using the last bit of plain buttercream, add a white triangle inside each eye.

TIP   *If you don't have piping tips, frost the cake with an icing spatula with the reddish-orange buttercream for a smooth cake instead of one with textured "fur," then finish with the face details.*

Transform simple chocolate cupcakes into an all-time favorite ice cream flavor: cookies and cream. By sandwiching luscious cream cheese frosting flecked with chocolate cookie crumbs between the cupcake's layers, it even looks like a chocolate cream sandwich cookie.

COOKIES & CREAM CUPCAKES

2 cups (10 oz/315 g) all-purpose flour

1 cup (3 oz/90 g) unsweetened cocoa powder

1 teaspoon baking powder

1 teaspoon baking soda

½ teaspoon kosher salt

2 cups (1 lb/500 g) sugar

1 cup (250 ml) canola oil

2 large eggs

1 tablespoon pure vanilla extract

1 cup (8 oz/250 g) sour cream

1 recipe Cream Cheese Frosting (page 101)

1¼ cups (3¾ oz/110 g) chocolate cookie crumbs (cream filling removed)

12 chocolate sandwich cookies, broken in half, for toppings

Makes 24 cupcakes

Place 1 rack in the upper third and 1 rack in the lower third of the oven and preheat to 350°F (180°C). Line 24 standard muffin cups with paper liners. In a bowl, sift together the flour, cocoa powder, baking powder, baking soda, and salt. Set aside.

In the bowl of a stand mixer fitted with the paddle attachment, beat together the sugar, oil, eggs, vanilla, and ½ cup (125 ml) water on medium speed until combined. Reduce the speed and add the flour mixture in 3 additions, alternating with the sour cream and beginning and ending with the flour, and beat until combined.

Divide the batter among the prepared muffin cups, filling them three-fourths full. (Don't fill less than three-fourths full because you want the cupcakes to form a dome when baking.) Bake until the tops of the cupcakes have formed a crust but still spring back when lightly touched and a toothpick inserted into the center comes out clean, 20–25 minutes, rotating the pans between the racks halfway through baking. Transfer the pans to wire racks and let cool for10 minutes. Remove the cupcakes from the pans and let cool completely on the racks.

Make the cream cheese frosting. After beating in the cream, add the cookie crumbs and beat until well combined, about 30 seconds. Transfer to a large pastry bag fitted with a large closed star tip.

Slice off the cupcake tops right where they meet the paper liners and reserve the cake tops. Pipe a layer of frosting around the outside edge of each cupcake, then cover with a reserved cupcake top. Pipe a dollop of frosting in the centerof each cupcake, top with a cookie piece, and serve.

PARTY WORTHY
These sculptural cupcakes
are an impressive finale
for any celebration.

THE PERFECT SHAPE
You can use a Bundt pan in place of a savarin mold. The cake will look different but will taste just as wonderful.

The ultimate birthday cake for any doughnut lover, without all the fuss of deep-frying. A savarin mold helps you create a ring-shaped cake easily. The frosting, pink-dyed marzipan, plus plenty of sprinkles, make it look like a real doughnut.

VANILLA DOUGHNUT CAKE

½ recipe Marzipan (page 90), tinted with pink food coloring

1 recipe Yellow Cake (page 94)

Unsalted butter, for greasing

1 recipe Doughnut Cake Buttercream (page 98)

Confectioners' sugar, for dusting

1 teaspoon light corn syrup

Rainbow sprinkles, for decorating

Serves 12–16

Make the marzipan as directed and refrigerate. Make the yellow cake batter. Preheat the oven to 375°F (190°C).

Pour half of the batter into an ungreased 10-inch (25-cm) round savarin (or Bundt) pan with a 7-cup (1.75-l) capacity and spread evenly. Set the remaining batter aside. Bake until a toothpick inserted into the center of the cake comes out clean, about 35 minutes. Transfer the pan to a wire rack to cool for 10 minutes, then invert the cake onto the rack and let cool completely. Wash and dry the pan, then repeat to bake the remaining batter.

Make the buttercream as directed. Using a serrated knife, cut off the top of each cake to create a flat surface. Using a spoon, scoop out a trench through the center of each cake about 1 inch (2.5 cm) wide. Transfer the pink buttercream to a pastry bag without a tip and pipe the buttercream into the trench. Using the back of a spoon, push the buttercream into the trench so that it fills up the space. Place one cake half on top of the other cake, cut sides facing in, to form a doughnut shape. Spread a thin layer of the light brown buttercream all over the cake.

Freeze for 10 minutes, then spread the remaining light brown buttercream over the cake. Dip a rubber spatula into hot water, shake off the excess, and smooth out the buttercream.

Using a pencil, trace the shape of your pan onto a sheet of parchment paper, then cut it out to make a template. Dust a work surface with confectioners' sugar. Roll out the marzipan slightly larger than the template, place the template on the dough, and cut wavy edges close to the edge of the template to resemble drips. Carefully place the marzipan on the cake. In a small bowl, stir together the corn syrup and 1 teaspoon water. Lightly brush the mixture over the marzipan, decorate with sprinkles, and serve.

Anyone who is a fan of Girl Scout cookies will recognize this beloved flavor combination. In a riff on one of their most popular cookie varieties, this moist coconut sheet cake is topped with a thick layer of caramel buttercream, plenty of toasted coconut, and a drizzle of dark chocolate.

COCONUT, CARAMEL & CHOCOLATE SHEET CAKE

FOR THE CAKE

6 tablespoons (3 oz/90 g) unsalted butter, at room temperature, plus more for greasing

2¾ cups (14 oz/440 g) all-purpose flour, plus more for dusting

2½ teaspoons baking powder

¾ teaspoon baking soda

¾ teaspoon kosher salt

3 large egg whites plus 1 large egg

2 cups (1 lb/500 g) granulated sugar

6 tablespoons (90 ml) coconut oil, at room temperature

1 teaspoon pure vanilla extract

1 cup (250 ml) coconut milk

½ cup (125 ml) buttermilk

To make the cake, preheat the oven to 350°F (180°C). Grease a 9-by-13-inch (23-by-33-cm) baking pan, line the pan with parchment paper, then grease the parchment. Dust with flour, then tap out any excess.

In a bowl, sift together the flour, baking powder, baking soda, and salt. Set aside. In the bowl of a stand mixer fitted with the whisk attachment, beat together the egg whites and 1 cup (8 oz/250 g) of the granulated sugar on medium-high speed until soft peaks form, about 3 minutes. Set aside.

In the clean bowl of the stand mixer fitted with the paddle attachment, beat together the butter, coconut oil, and the remaining 1 cup (8 oz/250 g) granulated sugar on medium speed until light and fluffy, about 2 minutes. Add the egg and vanilla and beat until combined, about 1 minute. Stop the mixer and scrape down the sides of the bowl. With the mixer on low speed, add the flour mixture in 3 additions, alternating with the coconut milk in 2 additions and the buttermilk in 1 addition. Beat until well combined. Raise the speed to high and beat for 30 seconds. Stop the mixer and scrape down the sides of the bowl.

FOR DECORATING

1 recipe Caramel-Coconut
Frosting (page 100)

1 cup (4 oz/125 g) shredded
dried unsweetened coconut,
toasted

6 oz (185 g) semisweet
chocolate, chopped

1½ teaspoons vegetable
shortening

Serves 15–18

Using a rubber spatula, gently fold the egg white mixture into the butter mixture until completely incorporated, taking care not to deflate the peaks. Transfer the batter to the prepared baking pan and spread evenly. Bake until a toothpick inserted into the center of the cake comes out clean, about 35 minutes. Transfer the pan to a wire rack and let cool for 15 minutes, then invert the cake onto the rack and let cool completely

Make the caramel-coconut frosting as directed. Spread the frosting over the top and sides of the cake. Sprinkle the top of the cake with half of the coconut, then press the remaining coconut onto the sides. In a heatproof bowl set over but not touching barely simmering water in a saucepan, combine the chocolate and shortening. Heat, stirring often, until melted, about 4 minutes. Transfer the chocolate mixture to a pastry bag and cut a small hole. Drizzle the chocolate over the cake in the desired pattern. The cake can be stored in an airtight container at room temperature for up to 2 days.

You don't need a special pan to create a heart-shaped cake for your Valentine. Here, we show you how to use round and square cake pans to make a scrumptious espresso-infused chocolate cake in the shape of a heart. A thick layer of frosting and plenty of edible flowers or sprinkles provide the finishing touch.

CHOCOLATE ESPRESSO VALENTINE'S HEART CAKE

FOR THE CAKE

½ cup (125 ml) canola oil, plus more for greasing

2½ cups (12½ oz/390 g) all-purpose flour, plus more for dusting

1 cup (3 oz/90 g) unsweetened cocoa powder

1½ teaspoons *each* baking powder, baking soda, and kosher salt

2 cups (1 lb/500 g) sugar

3 large eggs

1½ cups (375 ml) buttermilk

1 tablespoon pure vanilla extract

6 oz (185 g) semisweet chocolate chips, melted and cooled

4 teaspoons espresso powder

FROSTING OPTIONS

For a pink cake: 1 recipe Quick Vanilla Buttercream (page 97), tinted with red food coloring

For a double chocolate cake: 1 recipe Chocolate Frosting (page 100)

Edible flowers or rainbow sprinkles, for decorating

Serves 12–16

To make the cake, preheat the oven to 350°F (180°C). Grease an 8-inch (20-cm) round cake pan and an 8-inch (20-cm) square cake pan, line the bottoms of the pans with parchment paper, then grease the parchment. Dust with flour, then tap out any excess.

In a bowl, sift together the flour, cocoa powder, baking powder, baking soda, and salt. Set aside.

In the bowl of a stand mixer fitted with the paddle attachment, beat together the sugar, eggs, buttermilk, oil, and vanilla on medium speed until blended, about 2 minutes. Reduce the speed to low, slowly add the flour mixture, and beat until incorporated, stopping the mixer to scrape down the sides of the bowl as needed. Add the melted chocolate and espresso powder and beat until combined. Raise the speed to high and beat for 30 seconds.

Divide the batter evenly between the prepared pans and spread evenly. Bake until a toothpick inserted into the center of the cakes comes out clean, 30–35 minutes. Transfer the pans to wire racks and let cool for 10 minutes, then invert the cakes onto the racks and let cool completely.

To assemble, cut the round cake in half crosswise. Orient the square cake as a diamond. Frost the cut sides of the half rounds with buttercream or chocolate frosting and place them against the top sides of the diamond to form a heart shape, pressing gently to adhere. Spread the remaining buttercream or frosting over the entire surface of the cake. Decorate as desired with edible flowers or sprinkles and serve.

EXPRESS YOURSELF
Reserve some of the
frosting to pipe an extra
sweet message to your
valentine.

CHRISTMAS CLASSIC
With their wintry scenes,
these festive log-shaped
cakes are a holiday favorite.

This traditional holiday cake is created from a chocolate and whipped cream roulade, or rolled cake, decorated to look like a log. The finished cake takes some time, but it makes a fun family project. The little marzipan and sliced almond pinecones are simple to make and, along with sprigs of rosemary and a dusting of confectioners' sugar, add a charming woodland touch.

BÛCHE DE NOËL

½ recipe Marzipan (page 90)

FOR THE CAKE

⅓ cup (80 ml) canola oil, plus more for greasing

1⅔ cups (8½ oz/265 g) all-purpose flour, plus more for dusting

⅔ cup (2 oz/60 g) unsweetened cocoa powder

1 teaspoon baking powder

1 teaspoon baking soda

1 teaspoon kosher salt

1⅓ cups (11 oz/345 g) granulated sugar

2 large eggs

1 cup (250 ml) buttermilk

2 teaspoons pure vanilla extract

¼ lb (125 g) semisweet chocolate chips, melted and cooled

¾ teaspoon espresso powder

Make the marzipan as directed and refrigerate; do not roll out the dough.

To make the cake, preheat the oven to 350°F (180°C). Grease a rimmed sheet cake pan, line the pan with parchment paper, then grease the parchment. Dust with flour, then tap out any excess.

In a bowl, sift together the flour, cocoa powder, baking powder, baking soda, and salt. Set aside.

In the bowl of a stand mixer fitted with the paddle attachment, beat together the granulated sugar, eggs, buttermilk, oil, and vanilla on medium speed until blended, about 2 minutes. Reduce the speed to low, slowly add the flour mixture, and beat until incorporated, stopping the mixer to scrape down the sides of the bowl as needed. Add the melted chocolate and espresso powder and beat until combined. Raise the speed to high and beat for 30 seconds.

Transfer the batter to the prepared cake pan and spread evenly. Bake until a toothpick inserted into the center of the cake comes out clean, about 20 minutes. Transfer the pan to a wire rack and let the cake cool for 15 minutes, then place a clean tea towel over the top of the cake. Invert the cake and towel onto a cutting board and peel off the parchment from the cake bottom. Starting at the short end of the cake, gently roll the cake away from you, rolling the towel as you go, until you form a log. Let cool until just barely warm, about 20 minutes.

Continued on page 80

Continued from page 79

BÛCHE DE NOËL

2 recipes Classic Whipped Cream (page 91)

1 recipe Chocolate Frosting (page 100)

½ cup (2 oz/60 g) sliced almonds

4 fresh rosemary springs, for garnish

Confectioners' sugar, for dusting

Serves 12

Make the whipped cream and chocolate frosting.

Carefully unroll the cake and remove the tea towel. Spread the whipped cream evenly over the top of the cake, then reroll the cake. Using an offset spatula, spread the chocolate ganache frosting evenly over the rolled cake, then use the end of the spatula to create ridges and lines to look like tree bark.

To make the pinecones, using your hands, roll about ½ tablespoon of the marzipan dough into a ball. Starting at the bottom and working your way up, insert some of the almonds into the marzipan, creating a layered effect. Repeat with the remaining marzipan and almonds. The pinecones can be stored in an airtight container in the refrigerator for up to 1 day.

Decorate the cake with the pinecones and rosemary sprigs, dust with confectioners' sugar, and serve.

TIP *Roll the log slowly, using even pressure on both sides to prevent cracking. If the roll does crack, the whipped cream filling will hold the cake together. Refrigerate for 10 minutes before frosting with the ganache.*

Chocolate and peppermint make great flavor partners and this tall masterpiece of a cake makes full use of them. Crushed candy canes serve two purposes: to add flavor and texture to the buttercream filling and to decorate the outside of the cake in a fun and festive way.

PEPPERMINT DEVIL'S FOOD CAKE

⅔ cup (5 oz/155 g) unsalted butter, at room temperature, plus more for greasing

1¾ cups (9 oz/280 g) all-purpose flour, plus more for dusting

1 cup (250 ml) hot brewed coffee

¾ cup (2¼ oz/65 g) unsweetened cocoa powder

1½ teaspoons baking soda

1 teaspoon kosher salt

2 cups (1 lb/500 g) sugar

3 large eggs

1½ teaspoons peppermint extract

1 teaspoon pure vanilla extract

1¼ cups (310 ml) buttermilk

2 recipes Traditional Vanilla Buttercream (page 97)

1 teaspoon peppermint extract

1½ cups (4½ oz/135 g) crushed candy canes or peppermint candies

Serves 12

Preheat the oven to 350°F (180°C). Grease two 8-inch (20-cm) round cake pans, line the bottoms of the pans with parchment paper, then grease the parchment. Dust with flour, then tap out any excess.

In a small bowl, whisk together the coffee and cocoa powder until no lumps remain. In a medium bowl, sift together the flour, baking soda, and salt. Set aside.

In the bowl of a stand mixer fitted with the paddle attachment, beat together the butter and sugar on medium speed until light and fluffy, about 2 minutes. Add the eggs one at a time, beating until incorporated after each addition, then add the peppermint and vanilla extracts and beat until combined, about 1 minute. Reduce the speed to low and add the flour mixture in 3 additions, alternating with the buttermilk, beginning and ending with the flour. Beat in the last addition just until the flour disappears, about 30 seconds. Add the coffee mixture and beat until uniformly combined.

Divide the batter evenly between the prepared pans and spread evenly. Bake until a toothpick inserted into the center of the cakes comes out clean, about 40 minutes. Transfer the pans to wire racks and let cool for 10 minutes, then invert the cakes onto the racks and let cool completely.

Continued on page 82

Continued on page 82

Continued from page 81

PEPPERMINT DEVIL'S FOOD CAKE

Make the traditional vanilla buttercream; for each batch, replace ½ teaspoon of the vanilla extract with ½ teaspoon peppermint extract. Stir ¾ cup (2¼ oz/68 g) of the crushed candy canes into 1 batch.

To assemble the cake, using a large serrated knife, cut each cake in half horizontally to create 4 thin layers. Place the bottom layer on a cake stand or serving plate. Spread one-third of the candy cane buttercream evenly over the cake. Repeat with the remaining cake layers. Cover the entire cake with a crumb coat of peppermint buttercream and refrigerate for 30 minutes. Spread the remaining peppermint buttercream over the top and sides of the chilled cake. Press the remaining ¾ cup (2¼ oz/68 g) crushed candy canes against the sides and serve.

TIP *For best results, seal the candy canes in a lock-top plastic bag and crush with a frying pan or rolling pin to the desired texture.*

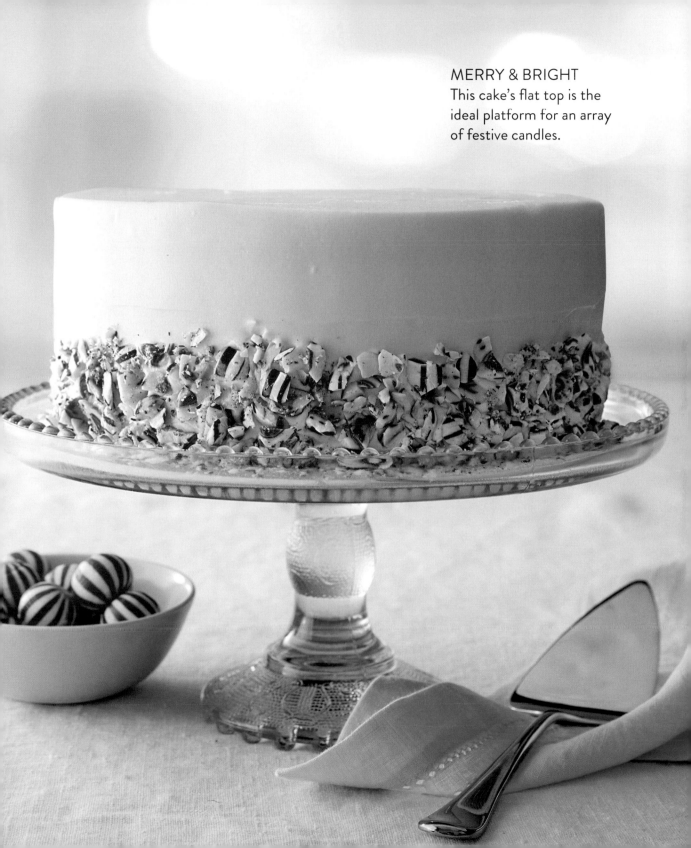

MERRY & BRIGHT
This cake's flat top is the
ideal platform for an array
of festive candles.

SNOWY COOKIES
Dust the remaining gingerbread cookies with confectioners' sugar.

The addition of Guinness stout and dark molasses gives this triple-layer gingerbread cake rich, dark flavor. But what really sets this dessert up for the holidays are the cutout gingerbread cookie decorations, rosemary sprig "trees," and a snowy dusting of confectioners' sugar. Get a head start by making the cookies and cake a day in advance, then assemble just before serving.

GINGERBREAD CAKE WITH MAPLE-MASCARPONE WHIPPED CREAM

FOR THE GINGERBREAD COOKIES

4 tablespoons (2 oz/60 g) unsalted butter, at room temperature

¼ cup (2 oz/60 g) firmly packed light brown sugar

3 tablespoons molasses

1 large egg yolk

1 cup (5 oz/155 g) all-purpose flour, plus more for dusting

¼ teaspoon baking soda

⅛ teaspoon kosher salt

1 teaspoon ground ginger

¼ teaspoon ground cinnamon

¼ teaspoon ground allspice

¼ teaspoon ground cloves

To make the gingerbread cookies, in the bowl of a stand mixer fitted with the paddle attachment, beat together the butter and brown sugar on medium speed until light and fluffy, about 2 minutes. Add the molasses and egg yolk and beat until combined, stopping the mixer to scrape down the sides of the bowl as needed. Reduce the speed to low and add the flour, baking soda, salt, ginger, cinnamon, allspice, and cloves. Beat until combined, then raise the speed to medium and beat until a thick dough forms, about 1 minute. Turn the dough out onto a lightly floured work surface and shape into a disk. Wrap in plastic wrap and refrigerate for at least 1½ hours or up to 3 days.

Preheat the oven to 350°F (180°C). Line a baking sheet with parchment paper.

Let the dough stand at room temperature for about 20 minutes. On a lightly floured surface, roll out the dough ¼ inch (6 mm) thick. Using cookie cutters, cut out desired shapes, such as trees, snowmen, and gingerbread men, and transfer to the prepared baking sheet, spacing them about 2 inches (5 cm) apart. Bake until the edges of the cookies are set, 6–12 minutes, depending on their size. Transfer the cookies to wire racks and let cool completely.

To make the cake, keep the oven set at 350°F (180°C). Grease three 8-inch (20-cm) round cake pans, line the bottoms of the pans with parchment paper, then grease the parchment. Dust with flour, then tap out any excess.

Continued on page 86

Continued from page 85

GINGERBREAD CAKE WITH MAPLE-MASCARPONE WHIPPED CREAM

FOR THE CAKE

¾ cup (180 ml) canola oil, plus more for greasing

2 cups (10 oz/315 g) all-purpose flour, plus more for dusting

1 cup (250 ml) Guinness or oatmeal stout

¾ cup (8¼ oz/260 g) molasses

½ teaspoon baking soda

3 large eggs

1 teaspoon pure vanilla extract

1 cup (8 oz/250 g) granulated sugar

1 cup (7 oz/220 g) firmly packed light brown sugar

1½ teaspoons baking powder

1 teaspoon salt

3 tablespoons ground ginger

3 teaspoons ground cinnamon

½ teaspoon ground cloves

½ teaspoon ground nutmeg

¼ teaspoon ground cardamom

1 recipe Mascarpone Whipped Cream (page 91)

1 teaspoon maple extract

4 fresh rosemary sprigs

Confectioners' sugar, for dusting

Serves 12

In a large saucepan over medium heat, combine the Guinness and molasses and bring to a boil. Remove from the heat and whisk in the baking soda. The mixture will bubble; continue to whisk until the bubbling subsides. Let cool completely.

In a large bowl, whisk together the eggs, vanilla, both sugars, and oil. Sift the flour, baking powder, salt, ginger, cinnamon, cloves, nutmeg, and cardamom over the egg mixture. Using a rubber spatula, fold until well combined into a cohesive batter. Add the Guinness mixture and stir until blended. The batter will be thin.

Divide the batter evenly among the prepared pans. Bake until a toothpick inserted into the center of the cakes comes out with just a few moist crumbs attached, 22–26 minutes. Transfer the pans to wire racks and let cool for 10 minutes, then invert the cakes onto the racks and let cool completely.

Make the mascarpone whipped cream, adding the maple extract along with the vanilla.

To assemble the cake, place 1 cake layer on a cake stand or serving plate. Spread one-third of the mascarpone whipped cream evenly over the cake. Repeat with the remaining cake layers, then spread the remaining whipped cream over the top of the cake. Gently stand the gingerbread cookies on top of the cake. Surround with the rosemary sprigs to resemble trees and dust the entire cake with confectioners' sugar to resemble snow. The cake can be stored in an airtight container in the refrigerator for up to 2 days.

Here, rich pumpkin cheesecake gets a lift from sweet bourbon and plenty of warm spices. This cheesecake would be a welcome finale to a festive holiday meal. Bonus! You can make the cheesecake a day in advance—in fact, it's even better the next day.

BOURBON PUMPKIN CHEESECAKE

FOR THE CRUST

7 oz (220 g) graham crackers

2 tablespoons firmly packed light brown sugar

⅔ cup (5 oz/155 g) unsalted butter, melted and cooled

Pinch of kosher salt

FOR THE FILLING

1 can (15 oz/470 g) pumpkin purée

2 large eggs plus 2 large egg yolks

½ cup (3½ oz/105 g) firmly packed light brown sugar

⅓ cup (80 ml) bourbon

3 tablespoons heavy cream

2 tablespoons fresh lemon juice

1 vanilla bean, split and seeds scraped, seeds reserved

1 tablespoon cornstarch

¼ teaspoon kosher salt

2 teaspoons ground cinnamon

1 teaspoon *each* ground ginger and nutmeg

1½ lb (750 g) cream cheese, at room temperature

1 recipe Classic Whipped Cream (page 91)

Serves 12

To make the graham cracker crust, in a food processor, pulse the graham crackers until the texture resembles sand. Add the brown sugar, melted butter, and salt and pulse until the texture resembles wet sand. Gently press the crust mixture evenly into the bottom and up the sides of a 9-inch (23-cm) springform pan. Refrigerate for 1 hour.

Preheat the oven to 350°F (180°C). To make the filling, in a bowl, whisk together the pumpkin purée, eggs, egg yolks, brown sugar, bourbon, cream, lemon juice, and vanilla bean seeds. Set aside.

In the bowl of a stand mixer, using a handheld whisk, whisk together the cornstarch, salt, cinnamon, ginger, and nutmeg. Add the cream cheese, then attach the bowl to the mixer fitted with the paddle attachment and beat on medium-high speed until smooth, about 3 minutes. Stop the mixer and scrape down the sides of the bowl. Add the pumpkin mixture and beat on low speed until blended, about 3 minutes.

Pour the filling into the chilled crust and place the pan on a baking sheet. Bake until the center is just set, 50–60 minutes. Transfer the pan to a wire rack and let cool to room temperature, then refrigerate until firm, at least 4 hours and preferably overnight. Remove the outer ring of the pan.

Just before serving, make the whipped cream and spread it over the chilled cheesecake, then serve.

BASIC RECIPES

LEMON CURD

8 large egg yolks

1½ cups (6 oz/180 g) sugar

2 tablespoons grated
lemon zest

¾ cup (180 ml) fresh lemon
juice

¾ cup (6 oz/180 g) cold
unsalted butter, cut into pieces

Makes 1 cup (250 ml)

In a saucepan over medium heat, combine the egg yolks, sugar, and lemon zest and juice. Cook, whisking often, until the mixture is thick enough to coat the back of a spoon, about 10 minutes. Add the butter and cook, stirring often, until melted, about 3 minutes. Reduce the heat to low and cook, whisking constantly, until it starts to thicken, about 1 minute longer. Strain the lemon curd through a fine-mesh sieve into a bowl. Cover and refrigerate for at least 2 hours or up to 3 days.

VARIATION | To make lime curd, substitute an equal amount of lime zest and juice for the lemon.

MARZIPAN

1½ cups (5 oz/120 g)
super-fine almond flour,
plus more as needed

1½ cups (6 oz/185 g)
confectioners' sugar, plus
more as needed

2 teaspoons almond or pure
vanilla extract

1 teaspoon rose water
(optional)

1 large egg white

Food coloring as desired
(optional)

Makes about ¾ lb (375 g)

In a food processor, combine the almond flour and confectioners' sugar and pulse until well combined. Add the extract, rose water (if using), and egg white and pulse until a thick dough forms. If the dough is wet and sticky to the touch, add 1–2 tablespoons more almond flour and pulse again. Add food coloring, if using, and pulse until evenly blended. If using more than one color, divide the dough into batches and dye separately. Turn the dough out onto a work surface and knead a few times. Shape into a disk, wrap in plastic wrap, and refrigerate for at least 1 hour or up to 1 month.

Let the dough stand at room temperature for about 5 minutes. Roll out the dough ¼ inch (6 mm) thick. If your rolling pin sticks to the dough, coat the pin very lightly with confectioners' sugar. Using a knife, cookie cutter, or pastry cutter, cut out the desired shapes and use right away.

MASCARPONE WHIPPED CREAM

⅔ cup (5 oz/155 g)
mascarpone cheese

1 cup (250 ml) heavy cream

¼ teaspoon pure vanilla extract

Makes about 4 cups (410 g)

In the bowl of a stand mixer fitted with the whisk attachment, beat together the mascarpone, cream, and vanilla on medium-high speed until stiff peaks form, about 3 minutes. Use right away, or cover and refrigerate for up to 2 hours.

VARIATION | To make Almond-Mascarpone Whipped Cream, add ½ teaspoon almond extract in place of the vanilla extract.

CLASSIC WHIPPED CREAM

1 cup (250 ml) heavy cream

¼ cup (2 oz/60 g) granulated sugar

1 teaspoon pure vanilla extract

Makes about 2 cups (310 g)

In the bowl of a stand mixer fitted with the whisk attachment, beat together the cream, granulated sugar, and vanilla on medium-high speed until soft peaks form, about 3 minutes. Use right away, or cover and refrigerate for up to 2 hours.

VARIATION | To make Frangelico Whipped Cream, add 2 tablespoons Frangelico in place of the vanilla extract.

WHITE CAKE

¾ cup (6 oz/185 g) unsalted butter, at room temperature, plus more for greasing

2¾ cups (14 oz/440 g) all-purpose flour, plus more for dusting

2½ teaspoons baking powder

¾ teaspoon baking soda

¾ teaspoon kosher salt

3 large egg whites plus 1 large egg

2 cups (1 lb/500 g) sugar

1 tablespoon pure vanilla extract

1½ cups (375 ml) buttermilk

Makes two to four round cake layers, one 9-by-13-inch (23-by-33-cm) sheet cake, or 24 cupcakes

Preheat the oven to 350°F (180°C). Grease two 8-inch (20-cm) round cake pans, line the bottoms of the pans with parchment paper, then grease the parchment. Dust with flour, then tap out any excess.

In a bowl, sift together the flour, baking powder, baking soda, and salt. Set aside. In the bowl of a stand mixer fitted with the whisk attachment, beat together the egg whites and 1 cup (8 oz/250 g) of the sugar on medium-high speed until soft peaks form, about 4 minutes. Set aside.

In the clean bowl of the stand mixer fitted with the paddle attachment, beat together the butter and the remaining 1 cup (8 oz/250 g) sugar on medium speed until light and fluffy, about 2 minutes. Add the egg and vanilla and beat until combined, about 1 minute. Stop the mixer and scrape down the sides of the bowl. With the mixer on low speed, add the flour mixture in 3 additions, alternating with the buttermilk and beginning and ending with the flour, and beat until combined. Stop the mixer and scrape down the sides of the bowl. Raise the speed to high and beat for 20 seconds.

Using a rubber spatula, gently fold the egg whites into the butter mixture until completely incorporated, taking care not to deflate the peaks. Divide the batter evenly between the prepared pans and spread evenly. Bake until a toothpick inserted into the center of the cakes comes out clean, 40–45 minutes. Transfer the pans to wire racks and let cool for 10 minutes, then invert the cakes onto the racks and let cool completely. The cakes can be stored in an airtight container at room temperature for up to 2 days.

VARIATION | Champagne Cake: Make the white cake batter, replacing the 1½ cups (375 ml) buttermilk with ¾ cup (180 ml) buttermilk and ¾ cup (180 ml) sparkling wine.

YELLOW CAKE

1 cup (8 oz/250 g) unsalted butter, at room temperature, plus more for greasing

3 cups (15 oz/470 g) all-purpose flour, plus more for dusting

2 teaspoons baking powder

¾ teaspoon baking soda

¾ teaspoon kosher salt

2 cups (1 lb/500 g) sugar

2 large eggs plus 2 large egg yolks

1 tablespoon pure vanilla extract

2 cups (500 ml) buttermilk

Makes two 8-inch (20-cm) round cakes, one 10-inch (25-cm) bundt cake, or one 9-by-13-inch (23-by-33-cm) sheet cake

Preheat the oven to 350°F (180°C). Grease two 8-inch (20-cm) round cake pans, line the bottoms of the pans with parchment paper, then grease the parchment. Dust with flour, then tap out any excess.

In a bowl, sift together the flour, baking powder, baking soda, and salt. Set aside.

In the bowl of a stand mixer fitted with the paddle attachment, beat together the butter and sugar on medium speed until light and fluffy, about 2 minutes. Add the eggs one at a time, and then the egg yolks and vanilla and beat until incorporated. Stop the mixer and scrape down the sides of the bowl. With the mixer on low speed, add the flour mixture in 3 additions, alternating with the buttermilk and beginning and ending with the flour and beat until combined. Stop the mixture and scrape down the sides of the bowl. Raise the speed to high and beat for 20 seconds.

Divide the batter evenly between the prepared pans and spread evenly. Bake until a toothpick inserted into the center of the cakes comes out clean, about 55 minutes. Transfer the pans to wire racks and let cool for 10 minutes, then invert the cakes onto the racks and let cool completely. The cakes can be stored in an airtight container at room temperature for up to 2 days.

CHOCOLATE CAKE

Nonstick cooking spray,
for greasing

½ cup (125 ml) canola oil,
plus more for greasing

1 cup (3 oz/90 g) unsweetened
cocoa powder, plus more
for dusting

2½ cups (12½ oz/390 g)
all-purpose flour

1½ teaspoons baking powder

1½ teaspoons baking soda

1½ teaspoons kosher salt

2 cups (1 lb/500 g) sugar

3 large eggs

1½ cups (375 ml) buttermilk

1 tablespoon pure vanilla extract

6 oz (185 g) semisweet
chocolate chips, melted and
cooled

1 teaspoon espresso powder

Makes two 8-inch (20-cm)
round cakes

Preheat the oven to 350°F (180°C). Grease two 8-inch (20-cm) round cake pans with cooking spray, line the bottoms of the pans with parchment paper, then grease the parchment and dust with cocoa powder.

In a bowl, sift together the flour, cocoa powder, baking powder, baking soda, and salt. Set aside.

In the bowl of a stand mixer fitted with the paddle attachment, beat together the sugar, eggs, buttermilk, oil, and vanilla on low speed until combined, about 2 minutes. Stop the mixer, add the flour mixture, and beat on low speed until combined, stopping the mixer to scrape down the sides of the bowl as needed. Add the melted chocolate and espresso powder and beat until combined. Raise the speed to high and beat for 20 seconds.

Divide the batter evenly between the prepared pans and spread evenly. Bake until a toothpick inserted into the center of the cakes comes out clean, 35–40 minutes. Transfer the pans to wire racks and let cool for 10 minutes, then invert the cakes onto the racks and let cool completely. The cakes can be stored in an airtight container at room temperature for up to 2 days.

TRADITIONAL VANILLA BUTTERCREAM

3 large egg whites

1 cup (8 oz/250 g) sugar

1 teaspoon pure vanilla extract

1 cup (8 oz/250 g) unsalted butter, at room temperature

Makes enough for one round layer cake or 12 mini layer cakes

Combine the egg whites and sugar in the bowl of a stand mixer and set over but not touching barely simmering water in a saucepan. Cook, whisking constantly, until the mixture is hot to the touch, about 160°F (71°C).

Attach the bowl to the stand mixer fitted with the whisk attachment, add the vanilla, and beat on medium-high speed until the mixture reaches room temperature, about 15 minutes. Switch to the paddle attachment, add the butter a few tablespoons at a time, and beat on low speed until incorporated. If the buttercream becomes grainy, raise the speed to high and beat until smooth, about 1 minute.

TIP   *Traditional buttercream is a more delicate frosting, so if you need to double the recipe, make two separate batches instead of one large batch.*

QUICK VANILLA BUTTERCREAM

2 cups (1 lb/500 g) unsalted butter, at room temperature

3 cups (12 oz/375 g) confectioners' sugar

2 teaspoons pure vanilla extract

⅛ teaspoon kosher salt

Makes enough for one round layer cake

In the bowl of a stand mixer fitted with the paddle attachment, beat the butter on medium speed until smooth, about 2 minutes. Add the confectioners' sugar, vanilla, and salt, raise the speed to medium-high, and beat until combined, stopping the mixer to scrape down the sides of the bowl as needed.

TIP   *Store buttercream in an airtight container at room temperature overnight or in the refrigerator for up to 3 days. If refrigerated, let stand at room temperature for about 1 hour before frosting your cake.*

COCONUT BUTTERCREAM

1 cup (8 oz/250 g) unsalted butter, at room temperature

½ cup (125 ml) coconut milk

4 cups (1 lb/500 g) confectioners' sugar

½ teaspoon pure vanilla extract

½ teaspoon coconut extract

⅛ teaspoon teaspoon salt

Makes enough for one 8-inch (20-cm) 3-layer cake

In the bowl of a stand mixer fitted with the paddle attachment, beat together the butter and coconut milk on medium speed until smooth, about 2 minutes. Add the confectioners' sugar, vanilla and coconut extracts, and salt, raise the speed to medium-high, and beat until combined, about 1 minute, stopping the mixer to scrape down the sides of the bowl as needed.

DOUGHNUT CAKE BUTTERCREAM

3 cups (1½ lb/750 g) unsalted butter, at room temperature

4½ cups (18 oz/560 g) confectioners' sugar

3 teaspoons pure vanilla extract

¼ teaspoon kosher salt

Pink, brown, and yellow food coloring, as needed

Makes enough for one 10-inch (25-cm) bundt cake

To make the buttercream, in the bowl of a stand mixer fitted with the paddle attachment, beat the butter on medium speed until smooth, about 2 minutes. Add the confectioners' sugar, vanilla, and salt, raise the speed to medium-high, and beat until combined, stopping the mixer to scrape down the sides of the bowl as needed. Transfer about one-fourth of the buttercream to a bowl, add 1 drop pink food coloring, and stir until combined. Add brown and yellow food coloring to the remaining batter until the desired light brown shade is reached.

CARAMEL-COCONUT FROSTING

¼ cup (2 oz/60 g) granulated sugar

4 tablespoons (60 ml) heavy cream, at room temperature

1 teaspoon pure vanilla extract

¾ teaspoon kosher salt

¾ cup (6 oz/185 g) unsalted butter, at room temperature

2 cups (8 oz/240 g) confectioners' sugar, sifted

1 cup (4 oz/125 g) shredded dried unsweetened coconut

Makes enough for one sheet cake

In a small saucepan, stir together the granulated sugar and 2 tablespoons water. Place over medium-high heat and bring to a boil. Cook without stirring until the mixture turns dark amber in color, about 6 minutes. Remove from the heat and slowly whisk in 1 tablespoon of the cream; the caramel will bubble and sputter. Whisk in the remaining 3 tablespoons cream, the vanilla, and salt until smooth. Let the caramel cool to room temperature, about 25 minutes.

In the clean bowl of the stand mixer fitted with the clean paddle attachment, beat the butter on medium-high speed until smooth, about 1 minute. Add the confectioners' sugar ¼ cup (1 oz/30 g) at a time and beat until light and fluffy, about 3 minutes. Stop the mixer and scrape down the sides of the bowl. Add the cooled caramel and beat on medium-high speed until thoroughly combined, about 2 minutes. Stop the mixer, add the coconut, and beat on low speed until combined, about 30 seconds.

TIP   *Watch carefully when making the caramel, as it can turn from perfectly caramelized to burnt in a matter of seconds.*

CHOCOLATE FROSTING

3 cups (18 oz/560 g) semisweet chocolate chips

3 cups (750 ml) heavy cream, plus more as needed

Makes enough for one round layer cake

Put the chocolate chips in the bowl of a stand mixer. Set aside. In a saucepan over medium-low heat, bring the cream to a simmer, about 3 minutes. Pour the hot cream over the chocolate and let stand for 10 minutes. Using a handheld whisk, whisk until the mixture is velvety and smooth and completely cooled.

Attach the bowl to the stand mixer fitted with the whisk attachment and beat on high speed until the frosting is light and fluffy, about 3 minutes. If it is too thick, beat in 1 tablespoon cream at a time until the desired consistency is reached.

MERINGUE FROSTING

1 ⅓ cups (11 oz/345 g) plus
2 tablespoons sugar

¼ teaspoon kosher salt

6 large egg whites

½ teaspoon cream of tartar

1 teaspoon pure vanilla extract

Makes enough for one
round layer cake

In a saucepan over medium-high heat, stir together the 1⅓ cups
(11 oz/345 g) sugar, salt, and ½ cup (125 ml) water and cook until
a candy thermometer registers 240°F (115°C).

In the bowl of a stand mixer fitted with the whisk attachment,
beat together the egg whites and cream of tartar on medium speed
until the mixture is foamy. Slowly add the 2 tablespoons sugar,
raise the speed to medium-high, and beat until medium-firm peaks
form. Reduce the speed to medium and slowly pour in the hot sugar
mixture, then raise the speed to high and beat until a thick, glossy
meringue forms, about 4 minutes. Add the vanilla and beat
for 1 minute.

TIP *Meringue frosting is best when used right away, although*
it can be covered and refrigerated for up for 1 day. Beat again
before using.

CREAM CHEESE FROSTING

1 cup (8 oz/250 g) unsalted
butter, at room temperature

3 cups (12 oz/375 g)
confectioners' sugar

½ teaspoon kosher salt

1 teaspoon pure vanilla extract

1 lb (500 g) cold cream cheese

2 tablespoons heavy cream

Makes enough for one round
layer cake or 24 cupcakes

In the bowl of a stand mixer fitted with the paddle attachment,
beat the butter on medium speed until smooth, about 1 minute.
Reduce the speed to low, add the confectioners' sugar, and beat until
combined, stopping the mixer to scrape down the sides of the bowl as
needed. Add the salt and vanilla and raise the speed to medium-high.
Add the cream cheese about 1 tablespoon at a time until combined
and no bits of cream cheese remain, about 2 minutes. Raise the speed
to high, add the cream, and beat until combined, 30–45 seconds.

TEQUILA CARAMEL SAUCE

½ cup (4 oz/125 g) unsalted butter

1 cup (7 oz/220 g) firmly packed light brown sugar

½ cup (125 ml) heavy cream

3 tablespoons (45 ml) tequila

Pinch of kosher salt

Makes enough for one 9-by-13-inch (23-by-33-cm) sheet cake

In a saucepan over medium heat, combine the butter and brown sugar and cook, whisking constantly, until the mixture thickens, about 5 minutes. Remove from the heat. Add the cream, tequila, and salt and whisk to combine. Return the pan to medium heat and cook until the caramel is thick enough to coat the back of a spoon, about 3 minutes, stirring occasionally. Transfer to a bowl and let cool completely.

RASPBERRY FILLING

3 cups (12 oz/375 g) frozen raspberries

⅓ cup (3 oz/90 g) sugar

2 teaspoons grated lemon zest

2 tablespoons fresh lemon juice

1 tablespoon cornstarch

Makes about 1 cup (10 oz/315 g)

In a saucepan over medium-high heat, combine the raspberries, sugar, lemon zest and juice, and cornstarch and bring to a simmer. Cook, stirring occasionally, until just beginning to thicken, about 2 minutes. Reduce the heat to low and cook, stirring occasionally, until the mixture is bubbling and thick enough to coat the back of a spoon, about 3 minutes. Transfer to a bowl and let cool completely. Store in an airtight container in the refrigerator for up to 1 week.

AMARETTO-POACHED PEARS

1½ cups (375 ml) amaretto

2 tablespoons firmly packed light brown sugar

2-inch (5-cm) strip lemon zest

Juice of 1 lemon

1 cinnamon stick

3 d'Anjou pears, peeled, halved, and cored

Makes enough to top one round layer cake

In a large saucepan over medium heat, combine the amaretto, brown sugar, lemon zest and juice, and cinnamon stick and bring to a simmer, whisking to dissolve the sugar. Add the pears and simmer, turning them over every 10 minutes if not completely submerged, until tender when pierced with a knife, about 1 hour. Let cool completely in the liquid, then remove from the liquid, reserving it if desired. Cut the pears lengthwise into slices about ½ inch (12 mm) thick or leave the halves whole.

TIP   *The pears can be refrigerated in the poaching liquid for up to 1 week; they will become more flavorful as they soak in the liquid.*

BROWN BUTTER GLAZE

3 tablespoons unsalted butter

¼ cup (2 oz/60 g) firmly packed light brown sugar

1½ tablespoons heavy cream

½ teaspoon kosher salt

Makes enough for one round layer cake

In a small saucepan over medium heat, melt the butter. Reduce the heat to medium-low and simmer gently, swirling the pan often, until the butter is toasty brown and smells nutty, 5–7 minutes. Add the brown sugar and whisk until combined. Continue to cook over medium heat, stirring occasionally, until thickened, about 4 minutes. Remove from the heat and stir in the cream and salt.

CANDIED BLOOD ORANGES

3 blood oranges, unpeeled, sliced into ⅛-inch (3-mm) rounds

2 cups (1 lb/500 g) sugar

2 tablespoons fresh orange juice

Makes enough to top one round layer cake

Fill a bowl half full with ice and water. Bring a saucepan of water to a boil over high heat. Add the orange slices and boil until softened, about 1 minute. Immediately transfer the slices to the ice bath and let cool completely, then drain.

In a frying pan over medium heat, combine the sugar, orange juice, and 2 cups (500 ml) water and bring to a boil, stirring until the sugar is dissolved. Reduce the heat to medium-low and add the orange slices in a single layer (you may have to do this in batches). Simmer until the rinds are slightly translucent, 45–60 minutes, turning the slices over every 15 minutes. Transfer the slices to a wire rack and let cool completely, at least 1 hour. The candied blood orange slices can be stored in an airtight container in the refrigerator for up to 1 month.

INDEX

FAVORITE CAKES

Conceived and produced by Weldon Owen, Inc.
In collaboration with Williams Sonoma, Inc.
3250 Van Ness Avenue, San Francisco, CA 94109

A WELDON OWEN PRODUCTION
P.O. Box 3088
San Rafael, CA 94912
www.weldonowen.com

WELDON OWEN INTERNATIONAL
President & Publisher Roger Shaw
SVP, Sales & Marketing Amy Kaneko

Associate Publisher Amy Marr
Senior Editor Lisa Atwood
Editor Alexis Mersel

Creative Director Kelly Booth
Art Director Marisa Kwek

Associate Production Director Michelle Duggan
Imaging Manager Don Hill

Photographer Sang An
Food Stylist Shelly Kaldunski
Prop Stylist Alessandra Mortola

Printed and bound in China

First printed in 2017
10 9 8 7 6 5 4

Library of Congress Cataloging-in-Publication
data is available.

ISBN: 978-1-68188-320-5

Additional photography on pages 10, 13, 19, 20-21, 25, 31, 32, 39, 49 (cake & cake slice),
70, 88, 93, 96 & 99 from photographer Annabelle Breakey, food stylist Abby Stolfo,
and prop stylist Emma Star Jensen.

ACKNOWLEDGMENTS

Weldon Owen wishes to thank the following people for their generous support
in producing this book: Emily Ayres, Lesley Bruynesteyn, Paul Davies, Penny Flood,
Tommy Fortier, Jackie Hancock, Kim Laidlaw, Eve Lynch, Rachel Lopez Metzger,
Sally Oanh Nguyen, Elizabeth Parson, and Emma Rudolph.